Simple Greenhouse Gardening

Simple Greenhouse Gardening

Edited by Francis Stark & Conrad Link

THE BOBBS-MERRILL COMPANY, INC.
Indianapolis • New York

Horticultural Consultants: Francis C. Stark, Professor and Chairman, Department of Horticulture, University of Maryland; and Conrad B. Link, Professor of Horticulture, University of Maryland. The section on vegetables was rewritten by Franklin D. Schales, Associate Professor of Horticulture, University of Maryland.

Cover photo courtesy of Lord & Burnham, Main Street, Irvington, New York 10533.

Contents

Introduction

Most books about greenhouse gardening assume that the reader is already an accomplished gardener and is familiar with the techniques of gardening. This book assumes that the reader knows practically nothing about greenhouses or gardening and takes him step by step through the stages of choosing a greenhouse, selecting a site, laying the foundations, putting it up, lighting it, heating it and maintaining it, and then goes on to describe the wealth of plants that can be grown in the greenhouse.

Simple Greenhouse Gardening contains, in simple, lucid terms, all the information an amateur needs to run a greenhouse with the minimum of effort and maximum of pleasure and satisfaction.

Roger Grounds

1 Greenhouse Structure and Design

Introducing the greenhouse — Construction materials — Greenhouse shape — Selecting a site — Foundations and erection — Maintenance — Heating a greenhouse — Ventilation and shading

Introducing the greenhouse

A greenhouse adds a new dimension to a garden. In it you can grow flowering plants, fruits, and vegetables that would perish outdoors in the cold winters of a temperate climate. Nor does it require a lot of time or expertise to get a great deal of enjoyment from a greenhouse. A gardener with a greenhouse can decide whether he is going to use it for growing exotic, tropical blooms; for forcing bulbs; for raising cuttings, seedlings, and summer bedding plants; or for growing tomatoes, lettuce, cucumbers, and other luscious fruits and vegetables. However, since there is a relationship between the type of greenhouse you buy and the sort of crops you can cultivate in it, first consider what type of greenhouse you want. Either decide what sort of plants you want to grow, and select a greenhouse suitable for the purpose; or decide what you can afford, and choose — as most people do — the best-value model in your price range.

Despite its mysterious reputation, greenhouse gardening is not difficult. There are no secrets to success. All you need do to run a greenhouse that will give you the greatest pleasure for the least effort is to decide what you want to do, find out the right way to do it, and then do it.

A temperate climate has many advantages to offer the outdoor gardener, but it also has its drawbacks: the majority of plants raised in the open have a growing season that lasts for little more than 4 to 8 of the 12 months of the year. Even then, the bulk of outdoor flowers bloom in the first 3 months of the summer, while most of the fruit crop is produced in the last 2 summer months. Some garden plants will flower outdoors in February or March, but they are few, and the vagaries of the weather are such that they may not always be very successful.

A greenhouse ameliorates the intemperance of the weather and enables you to grow special plants. Just how special these plants may be depends precisely on the lengths you are prepared to go to in controlling the environment within the greenhouse. This, in turn, is largely determined by what you are able to spend on both the greenhouse itself and on heating it. Plainly, the greater the degree of control you wish to exercise over the greenhouse's internal atmosphere, the more it will cost you.

Basically, there are four types of greenhouse to choose from, each maintained at a different temperature:

Cold greenhouses are heated solely by the sun. Although this restricts the house's usefulness to spring, summer, and fall, the results you get will depend a lot on where you live. Success will be greatest in sheltered, southerly spots, but even there the greenhouse will, except in abnormally mild winters, be useless for overwintering any plants that freeze at 32° F.

Cool greenhouses fit the needs and the pockets of many amateur gardeners. Unheated from late spring to fall, they are warmed artificially from late fall to spring to keep the temperature above 45° F. Being frost-free, the cool house is ideal for overwintering nonhardy plants and other garden stock.

Begonia "Firebrand." The tuberous-rooted begonias are among the most spectacular of the more easily grown greenhouse plants. They come in almost every color, single or double, many with frilled or picotee petals.

Intermediate or warm houses are kept at a heat never less than 55° F. This means that tomatoes, cucumbers, and cut flowers such as carnations and snapdragon can be raised in them. They are excellent for growing pot plants and for propagation.

Stove or hothouses, used for growing several kinds of orchids, tender plants, palms, and for high-temperature propagation, are heated so that they stay 65° F. or warmer.

Depending on the temperature, therefore, you will be able to grow a wide range of plants, shown in the following table. The cultivation of many of them is discussed in more detail in the second part of the book, but it is obvious that you do not, for example, need a hothouse to grow orchids or even intermediate temperatures to be successful with lettuce and azaleas.

4

COOL	INTERMEDIATE	HOT
Agapanthus	Adiantum	Aristolochia
Asparagus	Asplenium	Orchid
Azalea	Begonia	Palms
Cacti	Bougainvillea	Pineapple
Chrysanthemum	Carnation	
Cyclamen	Chrysanthemum	
Fuchsia	Cucumber	
Lettuce	Freesia	
Orchid	Gloxinia	
Rhubarb	Hyacinth	
	Lettuce	
	Mustard and cress	
	Orchid	
	Saintpaulia	
	Snapdragon	
	Tomato	
	Vines	

Construction materials

Before you buy a greenhouse, send for all the brochures you can, and read them thoroughly. You will then be in a good position to browse around a garden center or flower show before making a final choice. Remember that the more glass there is in the greenhouse in relation to solid materials, especially when there are no brick or composition base walls, the more heat the house will lose when there is no sunshine. This means that it is more expensive to keep an ''all-glass'' greenhouse at the temperature you want than it is to keep a greenhouse with brick half-walls at the desired temperature.

The vast majority of modern greenhouses are manufactured in prefabricated sections, although there is nothing to prevent a do-it-yourself enthusiast from building from scratch. How easy they are to erect depends on the detailed design, so it is worthwhile to find out in advance the time and trouble that will be involved in putting up a greenhouse of any particular type. The leading manufacturers deliver the complete greenhouse in sections and supply detailed erection instructions. When ordering a greenhouse, give the manufacturers a clear, precise order.

Aluminum, western red cedar, pressure-treated softwoods, and galvanized or enameled steel are the most common materials used for the framework of the greenhouse. They will need little maintenance. Many designs use putty on the sash bar and the glass pressed onto it and held in place with glazing nails. Alternatively, some designs use dry glazing, which involves sliding the glass into grooves, or clip-glaze by using metal clips to fit the glass onto a seal of plastic beading or bitumen. The following table gives a good idea of the features of various greenhouse materials.

MATERIAL	STRENGTH/ BULK RATIO	COST	DURABILITY
Redwood	Medium	Low	Good
Steel	Very high	Low	Rusts unless galvanized or painted regularly
Pressure-treated softwoods	Variable	Low	Good
Western Red Cedar	Low	Medium	Good
Reinforced concrete	Low	Medium	Good
Aluminum	High	Medium	Good

Light is all-important to plant growth, and this is especially true of greenhouse plants, many of which come from very sunny climates. Because light is so vital, ensure the best possible ratio between glass and framework in the greenhouse — but bear heating costs in mind.

Mini and Maxi. Two extremes in the size of greenhouses. 1. The Hall's Mini Greenhouse in red cedar. 2. A commercial greenhouse.

Greenhouse shape

The shape of your greenhouse will have an effect on the amount of light and heat reaching the plants within. The angle at which the sun's rays strike the ground — the angle of incidence — varies widely from summer to winter. Although in the north the days are longer in summer, the angle of incidence is smaller, and the sun's rays are less powerful. The more acute the angle of incidence, the less efficient your greenhouse will be, for the nearer the angle of incidence is to 90°, the more light and heat will get into the greenhouse. (See page 11).

GREENHOUSE TYPE	SPECIAL FEATURES	RANGE OF ACTIVITIES
SPAN-ROOFED (wood, alloy, steel)	Brick base wall	Pot plants, propagation, chrysanthemums in pots.
	Weatherboard base wall	Retain less heat, but base wall can be lined with insulating materials such as fiber glass.
	Glass to ground level	More costly to heat, but better light transmission makes them ideal for soil-grown crops.
LEAN-TO (Single pitch or ¾-span)	With or without base wall	Will grow most crops, but there can be problems with ventilation and overheating unless ventilating fans are installed. Light distribution unequal.
DUTCH LIGHT	Glass to ground level	Ideal for summer crops. Frequently used for lettuce and tomatoes. Much heat loss from loose glazing system.
CURVILINEAR	On small base wall or with glass to ground level	Both ideal for most activities. Heat loss fairly high with second type.

Crotons, properly known as *Codiaeum,* have the most fantastically colored leaves of any greenhouse plants. There are numerous named cultivars, each with differently patterned leaves. Those with narrow leaves will withstand lower temperatures than those with broad leaves.

CIRCULAR (or "Geodetic")	Still in fairly early stages of development	Particularly good for pot-plant culture and propagation. Fan ventilation or "air conditioning" is likely to be beneficial.
PLASTIC	"Do-it-yourself" type	Will grow most crops, provided crop support is adequate. Fan ventilation essential.
	Aluminum frame	Excellent for all activities. Fan ventilation is essential.

9

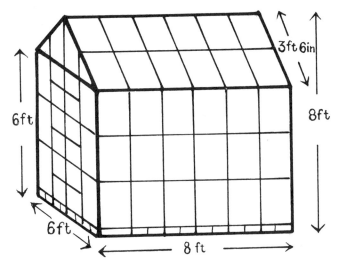

3ft 6in

6ft

8ft

6ft

8 ft

▲
Diagram showing how to calculate the area of glass through which heat is lost. Such calculations are necessary in order to find out how much heat must be put into the greenhouse to maintain any given minimum winter temperature.

Diagram showing how a large proportion of the sun's rays are deflected by the upper slope of a conventional span-roofed greenhouse.   ▶

A greenhouse with a conventional tent-shaped sloping roof will absorb light differently in different positions. If the length of the greenhouse runs east-west, during winter most of the sunlight will be deflected off the roof and absorbed through the vertical side walls. Once the sun gets higher in the sky, the south-facing slope of the roof will absorb radiation direct. Although sunlight will reach the back of the house, this does mean that a dense crop of plants on the south side of the greenhouse will shade any plants behind.

Turning the greenhouse so that it faces north-south will even out the light in summer but has the disadvantage that in winter only the south-facing gable can catch the light. An east-west set-up will probably suit most gardeners best, but it might be even more practical to select one of the new greenhouse designs with a semi-circular curved roof (a curvilinear greenhouse) or one completely circular in shape. These greenhouses, the result of experi-

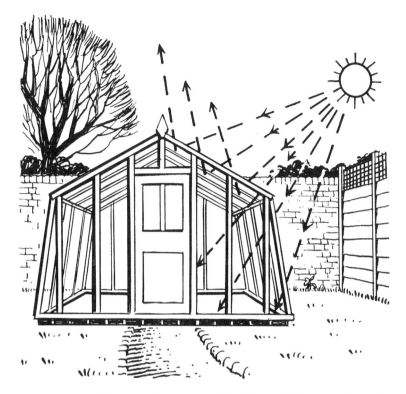

ments to find the best design for absorbing winter sun, function well all year when lined up east-west.

Greenhouses are often classified according to the shape of their roofs:

Span-roofed houses, the most popular kind, are tent-shaped and have sides that are either vertical or slightly sloping. The roof rises to a ridge in the center. The angle of the roof varies widely, but the slope is generally steeper when the panes of glass overlap than when they do not. If you live in a place that gets a lot of snow in winter, choose a more sloping roof. This will help avoid damage, especially if the house is unheated.

The size of a span-roofed greenhouse can vary from 6 x 4 ft. upward, but the most popular size is 6 x 8 ft., as this leaves room inside for two 3-ft. benches and a 2-ft. path or for two good-sized soil beds. The greenhouse glass can come down to the level of the

Types of Greenhouses
The traditional span-roofed type. This is most popular of all greenhouse designs. It has been tried and tested over a long period of time and can be relied on to give good all-around performance.

foundations, or the vertical walls may be built up for 2 to 3 ft. with brick or block. These base walls can also be of metal, plastic, wood, or asbestos cement. Some greenhouses have a base wall on one side and a glass front on the other, usually the south side, which is often an ideal compromise.

Gutters or eaves traverse the span-roofed greenhouse at between 4 and 6 ft., while the ridge itself is usually some 2 to 3 ft. higher. The roof is fitted with ventilators, and sometimes the sides, too, although these side vents are unnecessary if you decide to fit the greenhouse with an exhaust fan. In this case, ventilators need only serve as air inlets.

Lean-to houses, unpopular in the past because they were difficult to ventilate, became overheated in summer, and trapped little light in winter, are modern favorites because they are conve-

Lean-to greenhouse or conservatory. Greenhouses of this type are economical to operate, since heating can often be supplied from the domestic circuit. They are ideal where one wants to grow a vine up the back wall.

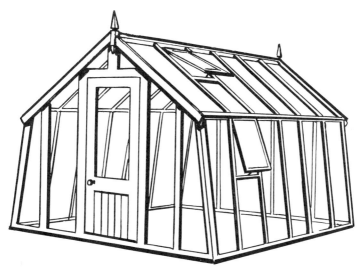

Dutch-type greenhouse. This type of greenhouse is best used for growing plants directly in the ground, and is particularly useful for growing tomatoes, lettuce, chrysanthemums, and cut flowers.

Angle of incidence of the sun's rays in summer. Note the high proportion of rays actually reaching the floor of the greenhouse.

nient to use and can be heated directly from the domestic heating circuit, particularly if house and greenhouse are built at the same time. New fan designs have solved the ventilation difficulties, and the lean-to house can be very successful if situated facing south. If it faces west, it might be best to employ it as a conservatory to catch the evening sun, while a north-facing lean-to is ideal for raising ferns and some alpines and shade-loving pot plants.

The roof of the lean-to can either be a single slope or a three-quarter pitch with a ridge. Unless you can use the extra height of a ridge to fit an additional ventilator above the top level of the back wall, and level with one on the opposite slope, it is probably not worth the extra expense. If you cannot afford exhaust fans, make sure that the ventilators on the sides and front of any lean-to give a good through-current of air. The construction of lean-to greenhouses is very similar to that of span-roofed shapes.

Sun porches, like lean-to greenhouses, can be very useful, particularly for growing pot plants. Their greatest disadvantage is that they tend to be drafty, so that plants are chilled as doors are constantly opened and shut.

Dutch light houses, Although greenhouses with glass reaching to ground level are often called "Dutch type," a true Dutch light greenhouse consists of single sheets of glass, each framed lightly in wood and measuring 5 x 2½ ft., which are then bracketed together by their grooved sides. The gable ends are hinged so that they can be lifted to make room for a tall crop. Popular with lettuce, tomato, and chrysanthemum growers, these greenhouses are not very good for an amateur, because their all-glass composition means a large heat loss and because warmth is also lost from between the frames, which have to be held loosely in place to prevent damage from the wind. But Dutch light greenhouses are inexpensive to buy and very easy to put up.

An average single-span Dutch light greenhouse will measure 12 to 13 ft. in width and about 8 ft. in height. The low roof does restrict head and working room, but it is possible to build the whole house onto a brick base wall.

Another modification used by professionals is to fit the greenhouse with pulley wheels so that it is mobile. Dutch light greenhouses on wheels are especially useful for simple rotation of crops. As a first experiment, you could use one to cover an early crop of lettuce until March or the first weeks of April, push it along to be a suntrap over a tomato crop in summer, and finally use it as a house for chrysanthemums in an adjacent plot which had been planted in May. The next year, the plants could be changed around so that each has a new site. However, mobility will add an extra 25 or 30 percent to the cost of a greenhouse that will already be expensive to heat and which takes up a lot of space.

The staging arrangements in the "Circulair" greenhouse. Note that there are three levels of staging. Those plants needing the most light can be grown on the highest level of staging, while those needing the least light can be grown on the lowest level. *Courtesy of Humex.*

The heating cables of the "Circulair" greenhouse provide for all-around warmth and ensure an even temperature in all parts of the greenhouse. *Courtesy of Humex.*

The geodetic greenhouse, still regarded by some as a gimmicky novelty, is in fact designed on the soundest scientific prinicples. *Courtesy of "Solardomes."*

Curvilinear, Quonset, or mansard houses, because they allow so much light to enter, make ideal all-purpose greenhouses. A house of this shape would be an excellent choice if you wanted to specialize in pot plants and propagation. Made of alloy or treated steel, they are extremely sturdy and are obtainable in many different sizes and in lean-to form.

Circular houses have only recently become available but are rapidly growing in popularity as their efficiency is being broadcast. A built-in air-conditioning system or exhaust fans are, however, a must, to prevent overheating in summer.

Plastic greenhouses, made of 2 mil. polyethylene or PVC polyvinyl chloride with rigid supports, although not ideal, are inexpensive, simple to construct, can be moved around the garden, and are improving in design every year. Plastic greenhouses come in many different shapes and sizes. Some, although rather flimsy, are designed so that you can build them yourself, while other, more sturdy types are obtainable ready-made. The most recent model is the "bubble" house, which is inflated with one fan and ventilated with another.

A greenhouse covered with plastic will probably last for one season or more, depending on the kind. Eventually, the ultraviolet rays from the sun weaken the material, and it is torn by the wind. Another disadvantage is that the plastic quickly becomes cloudy and dirty because dust clings to it. Although a plastic greenhouse will transmit light very efficiently, it will not, unlike glass, trap heat from the soil and from metal fittings, which means that it cools down very quickly. PVC, however, is slightly more effective than polyethylene.

Inside a plastic greenhouse, ventilation with electrically powered fans is essential to cut down condensation, and this will, of course, add to the cost. Remember to anchor the greenhouse firmly, and provide extra support for crops like tomatoes or cucumbers which are strung up on overhead wires.

Whatever their design, all greenhouses should be stable enough to withstand strong winds and constructed so that the panes of glass do not vibrate and shatter. When making your choice, see that the greenhouse door is conveniently placed and wide enough to take a wheelbarrow, and that it opens inward or slides back and forth. Try not to buy a house so small that you always have to stoop when inside. Small houses can be raised by placing them on several courses of bricks or blocks.

Selecting a site

The success of your greenhouse will depend a great deal on where you put it, for a convenient spot in the garden will be useless if it gets no sun. You should aim for a position that receives the maximum amount of sunshine both summer and winter — but remember to take into account the shade cast by trees and buildings and the variation in the angle of incidence of the sun's rays from June to December.

A perfect greenhouse site will be well sheltered, but the shelter will not cut down the light. Shelter is important because it cuts down the risk of damage from storms; it also cuts down heat loss. You will probably have to compromise between the protection it gives and a loss of sun for a short time each day. In very exposed areas, try to put the greenhouse between hedges planted to protect the house from prevailing cold winds. In some locations, protection may be needed on three sides.

Keep the greenhouse at least 10 to 15 ft. from a hedge to avoid overshading and interference from root growth. If trees are your shelter — like deciduous hedges they let light through in winter — double the distance. Solid walls are not a good idea: they stop the wind too sharply, deflecting it instead of breaking its force. Instead, choose an open fence, plastic mesh, or ''lattice'' wall.

Three other vital factors in selecting a site for your greenhouse are water, drainage, and electricity. A good supply of water is essential. Lay the permanent pipe underground to prevent freezing. Although you may be able to lay plastic pipes yourself, the job is probably best left to a qualified plumber.

Alternatives to a permanent pipe are the hose and the watering can or an underground pipe fixed temporarily to an outside hydrant. For the first of these methods, you will need a large hose, especially if you plan to use a spray or mist in the greenhouse as these need a good volume and pressure of water — about 40 to 60 lb. per sq. in. The temporary connection has the problem that water left in the pipes during winter may freeze and rupture the pipes.

Drainage is an aspect of greenhouse planning that is often ignored. A large amount of rainwater will collect in the gutters or run off the roof of a greenhouse. If the greenhouse has gutters linked to vertical pipes, connect these to a drain or to a seep hole, which is a gravel-filled drainage pit. Should the rain run straight onto the ground around the greenhouse, lay tile or gravel drains joining up with a convenient field drain outlet or seep hole. A barrel will collect a significant amount of rainwater, which you can use to advantage in other parts of the garden.

When planning your electricity supply, look ahead to the equipment you may acquire in future years. A light will use 100 watts of electric power, a heater 2½ kilowatts. Added to a soil-warming cable and possibly a mist irrigation unit, the total may be 4 or 5 kilowatts, which will mean you will need a heavy-gauge electric cable. All electrical fittings and cable-laying should be left to a qualified electrician, although you can do some of the preliminary work yourself.

Once you have made your own greenhouse plans, do not forget

A general view of a greenhouse, showing the range of decorative plants that can be grown. If a pond can be included, as it has been here, an even wider range of plants can be grown.

that you may need a building permit from your local authority. To be safe, it is worth submitting a scale plan, with the greenhouse position clearly marked in red, details of the dimensions (the manufacturer will supply plans, but you will have to draw these yourself if you are building your own greenhouse), and plans of the drains if they link up with the sewers.

A flat piece of land is, of course, the best place to start building a greenhouse, but it is well worth making the effort to level sloping ground thoroughly, particularly if you want to use the topsoil to make borders inside the house. The easiest time to level is when the soil is dry. This will prevent damaging its texture, and you can choose one of the following three methods.

Cut and fill. In this process, the topsoil is stripped from the site and stacked on one side. The site is leveled by moving the subsoil from the highest point to the lowest, and then replacing the topsoil. This simple procedure is excellent for a shallow slope, but on steeper ground you will run into drainage problems unless you build a retaining wall with a drain behind it to collect water running down from the higher ground.

If the topsoil is deep, you may not need to remove it. Whatever your method, do not be impatient. Wait for the soil to settle before you lay the greenhouse foundations. It is usually best to let the soil settle for a whole winter.

Leveling to the lowest point involves stripping off the topsoil, stacking it, removing the subsoil to the level you want, and then putting back the topsoil. While it is simple, this method can lead to drainage problems.

Leveling to the highest point is perhaps the best procedure, especially if the slope is acute, as it will solve most of your drainage difficulties. Use soil or gravel, depending on whether or not you want greenhouse borders, to raise the level. Add a wall at the base of the platform to keep the soil in place. The only disadvantage of this system is that drainage may be *too* efficient, and water may run too quickly from the ground beds. This is because the greenhouse is largely above the normal soil level.

Foundations and erection

The next step is to lay the greenhouse foundations, but before doing this you will need accurate measurements of the greenhouse. To avoid frustration, do wait until the greenhouse arrives, although delivery may take some weeks. Do not clutter up the site, but ask for the sections to be unloaded nearby. Then check the plans carefully; make sure that all the parts that should have been delivered have, in fact, arrived; and verify all the measurements, noting whether they are "outside to outside," "inside to inside," or "center to center."

Now peg out the exact position of the greenhouse. Rather than use odd pieces of scrap wood, take the trouble to cut inch-square

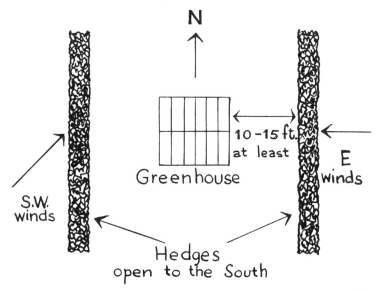

N

S.W. winds

Greenhouse

10 -15 ft. at least

E winds

Hedges open to the South

Diagram showing the siting of the greenhouse in relation to the points of the compass, to prevailing winds, and to windbreaks.

wooden pegs, 14 to 16 in. long and pointed at one end. Set one peg at the correct distance from the fence, house, or other landmark, and then, using a steel measuring tape, put the other end peg in position, also at the right distance away from the landmark so that the greenhouse is in line. You can use a compass to check the orientation of the greenhouse, although it does not matter if you are a few degrees away from direct north-south or east-west.

To ensure accuracy, measure from the center of each peg, and set the end pegs in exact positions, adding intermediate ones if the greenhouse is very long—kept in line by means of a tightly stretched cord. For a small greenhouse, a spirit level and a long, straight board will be quite sufficient to check the horizontal level. A large house may need more sophisticated transit or level, but you may require expert help to use this instrument.

Now comes the task of setting the width of the greenhouse at exact right angles to the length. The easiest way to do this is to make an accurate triangle with pieces of wood 3, 4, and 5 ft. long, checking the right angle formed with a rafter square. Set the corner

An exterior view of an all-glass greenhouse. Note how the brickwork has been used to create a level plinth for the greenhouse structure.

of this triangle exactly to the end stakes and support the other two corners with bricks. Using a line attached to the end stakes, form a right angle along the edge of the triangle. Measure along the line until you have the right width, and insert stakes. Check that the lengthwise distance is still correct, level up all the pegs, and tap a nail into the center of each corner peg. If you have a builder's site square, this will make really accurate right angles, although again you may need expert help to use it.

Finally, attach taut lines to the nails on each corner peg. This can be done by placing stout pegs 2 to 3 ft. outside the outline of the greenhouse. Then remove the corner pegs. By doing this, you will leave yourself plenty of room to maneuver, and the foundations can be worked without detracting from your accurate start and without having to work around the pegs.

The greenhouse supplier will tell you what sort of foundations you need to support a base wall or base blocks. Laying foundations should be no problem to the do-it-yourself expert, but it is important to bear in mind that firm anchorage to the ground is essential.

A sequence showing construction of the greenhouse from beginning to end. Note that a level site is needed before construction can begin.

3

4

5

6

Using the outside dimensions of the greenhouse as your guide, marked out with lines, dig a trench 5 to 6 in. deep and 12 to 14 in. wide if you are building a full 8-in. width brick wall, 8 to 9 in. wide if you plan a half-brick (4-in.) wall or are using 4-in. blocks. If you have just leveled the soil, you may need to dig deeper to pour the footing in undisturbed ground.

Mix the concrete for the footings, using three parts of gravel, two parts of sharp sand, and one part of cement. Run this in as a layer at least 4 to 6 in. deep, and use a straight board to make it level. According to the maker's directions, set in any necessary securing bolts at this stage. Once the footings have hardened, you can begin building up bricks or blocks, using a three-to-one mixture of sand and cement (measured by volume). Stick closely to the plans, so that the base wall keeps to the exact greenhouse dimensions. As the walls rise, do not forget to leave spaces for doors and ventilators. Check the vertical plumb of the walls frequently, using a spirit level and plumb line. If the base wall is very high or your site slopes slightly, you may need to reinforce it by hammering in steel rods.

The final part of the building will depend on your style of greenhouse, but full instructions are usually supplied. Large, modern prefabricated sections should present few difficulties. Popular glazing methods, as already mentioned (p. 6), include sealing strip with nonhardened bitumen and plastic "strip and clip." In Dutch light greenhouses, the glass slides into grooves. Always glaze on a dry day if you possibly can.

Maintenance

Although modern greenhouses need a mimimum of attention, there are some chores you cannot avoid. Red cedar can be left untreated, in which case it will mellow to silver-grey, or it can be treated with a cedar preservative, obtainable from hardware stores or from garden centers. If pressure-treated in advance, softwoods will last a long time without painting, although they are not very attractive.

Many small bulbs that flower in the depths of winter can be grown to perfection in a frost-free greenhouse. If grown outdoors their flowers would be ruined by winter weather.

Untreated softwoods will need regular painting to prevent weather damage. Either use white lead paint on top of a priming coat, or, if the wood can be cleaned with a wire brush, apply an aluminum paint, although it is not as attractive or long-lasting as its lead counterpart. If putty has been used for glazing, paint over it and add an eighth to a sixteenth of an inch of paintwork over the glass to give a good seal. Use masking tape to achieve a clean, straight line.

Painting both the outside and the inside of a greenhouse definitely increases the amount of light reflected into it. As an alternative, you can treat wood with a spirit-based perservative, but the job is best done before the house is erected, especially if it is part plastic. It costs very little to have wood pressure-treated before you buy the greenhouse, and this is even more effective. Aluminum houses need no painting, but steel greenhouses may eventually need painting, preferably with aluminum-based paint.

Even if you plan to paint them eventually, treat benches and shelves to begin with, using a spirit-based preservative. Because it gives off damaging fumes, especially when heated, *never* use creosote for this job. Products containing copper naphthenate are excellent and safe for plants.

Dirt is the great enemy of the greenhouse gardener. In towns and cities in particular, it sticks to the glass, both inside and out, and cuts down the amount of light passing through the glass. Cleaning the glass does not take very long. For the outside, use a proprietary cleaner or a solution of oxalic acid — one pound to a gallon of water. Spray it onto the glass and wash it off with a hose. Any good detergent will do to clean the inside, but remove the plants before you begin. Use a scraper to get rid of moss and algae growing over the glass, and wash them away with a jet of water. Moss is most likely to grow on the north side of a greenhouse, and, if it is prevalent, you may have to replace a few panes of glass occasionally.

Once a year give the inside of the base walls a good scrub and whitewash them. Give the heating pipes an occasional coat of aluminum paint. Contrary to popular belief, this will not impair their heating performance.

Heating a greenhouse

Heating an ordinary house and heating a greenhouse have much in common, yet it is easy to become confused because of all the talk about the efficiency of different methods. However, the science of heating is a precise science, and it is easy, once you know how, to calculate the cost and efficiency of each method.

A heating engineer will start an appraisal of a heating project by calculating the heat loss of a building. The first information needed is the heat-transmitting, and thus the heat-loss value of various materials. Known as the *thermal conductivities* of substances, these are measured in standard British thermal units (Btu's) and are universally accepted as follows:

	Heat conducted per sq. ft. per hour for every degree F.
Glass (including its framework)	1.1 Btu
4½-in. brick or composition block	0.5 Btu
Double brick wall, 9 in. thick	0.4 Btu
Wood, 1 in. thick	0.5 Btu
Asbestos (sheet or corrugated)	1.1 Btu
Concrete, 4 in. thick	0.75 Btu
Double-glazed glass (properly sealed)	0.5 Btu

This table shows that glass loses heat more than twice as fast as wood or brick, and that double glazing cuts heat loss by half. Technically speaking, heat is also lost through the floor, but this is usually ignored, as the ground area of the greenhouse often stores heat very effectively by reflecting it back into the greenhouse.

To calculate the heat loss of your own greenhouse, you must now measure up the total areas of glass and brick, cement or wood in square feet, and multiply each by the above value for thermal conductivity. The plan sheets are easiest to use for this.

Suppose the heat lost by a perfectly tight greenhouse, as an example, is 259 Btu's per hour. However, an average greenhouse is bound to have some leaks. A very exposed greenhouse will lose more heat than the norm, a sheltered one will lose less. A realistic addition to the heat loss is a third of the normal, giving here a figure of 343 Btu's.

Having made this calculation, you must now decide how much you want to heat the greenhouse. This will depend, of course, on where you live and what you want to grow. A greenhouse kept at 65° F. in all weather will need a "lift" of some 45 to 50° F. over the outside temperature, assuming that this may drop as low as 15 to 20° F. To work out the heat input, simply multiply the heat loss, in this case 343 Btu's by 45 or 50. For a temperate or intermediate house multiply by 35; for a cool house multiply by 20 or 25. As a sample calculation, 343 x 35 gives 12,005. This is the number of

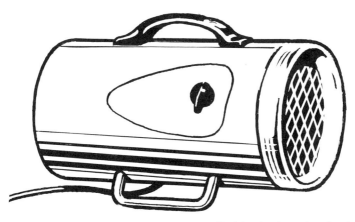

A through-flow-type electric greenhouse heater. Such heaters have the advantages of keeping the air in the greenhouse circulating and of ensuring that all parts are heated properly.

Btu's per hour needed to heat the intermediate greenhouse, whatever your heat supply, during the coldest weather.

However, these calculations represent the ideal. In practice there are several factors that can influence your heat equation. The most important of these concerns the properties of glass, for while glass is a first-rate transmitter of heat and the heat of the sun passes through it with ease, it is, at the same time, a poor insulator. This means that while glass, unlike plastic, can trap a large spectrum of the sun's heat waves, it cannot store heat for long. Once the temperature outside the greenhouse drops, glass will quickly transmit the heat back again. Two layers of plastic with an air space between makes a good insulated house.

Reducing the area of glass in your greenhouse will, of course, cut down this heat loss, but a great deal of warmth will be sacrificed unnecessarily if your greenhouse has badly fitting doors and ventilators or is poorly glazed. A high wind outside the house will step up the heat loss even more.

Double glazing is effective in reducing wasted heat because it traps a pocket of insulating air between two layers of sealed glass. Although costly, double-glazed greenhouses are on the market, but an alternative, albeit a rather crude one, is to line your greenhouse internally with plastic. If you do this, remember to leave the ventilators free, and bear in mind that you may need to install exhaust fans to cope with the increased condensation.

In a changeable climate artificial heating is the only way to keep a greenhouse at a reasonable temperature all year. The amount your heating will cost will depend on the fuel you choose, on the sophistication of the system — it could be automatic or semi-automatic to save you work and worry — and the efficiency of the heat-producing units. All systems waste some heat, usually through the flue pipes, but any reputable supplier will give you an accurate estimate of total costs.

There are three main methods of heating a greenhouse:

Hot pipes contain hot water which is, in turn, heated by a boiler fired by solid fuel, oil, gas, or electricity. The simplest boilers will need daily stoking, but some solid-fuel systems are semi-automatic. If you choose a new gas, oil, or electric boiler, then it will work on a completely automatic electric-powered time switch.

Oil heaters can be simple oil stoves that heat the air in the greenhouse direct, or they may consist of more complicated pressure jet or vaporized burners that heat air in perforated polyethylene pipes, possibly with the assistance of fans. Electricity is needed to work these fans and the pressure jet burners and can be used to control a thermostat system. Unsophisticated oil heaters must be regulated by hand.

Electrical heating systems come in several different designs, each ideal for automatic control:

Soil or bench-warming cables heat the growing medium but have little effect on the air temperature inside the greenhouse.

Fan heaters can be placed anywhere but work best in the center of the house. The largest fan heaters, however, are placed at one end of the greenhouse, and hot air is distributed through perforated polyethylene tubes.

Storage heaters are useful, but some experts discount them because they make the temperature difficult to control.

Once you have produced a high temperature inside your greenhouse, the next problem will be to distribute it evenly, particularly in cold weather. Hot-water pipes are the best by far. Transmitting heat by the convection currents of rising hot air, they can set up a warm curtain of air around the greenhouse. And by the process of radiation they warm the soil, a special bonus for heat-loving crops such as tomatoes. Benches, too, will benefit from hot-water pipes, but the pipes will only work efficiently if kept at the same temperature all along their length. Place the pipes around the edges of the greenhouse.

A heater that merely pumps out warm air from one spot is not ideal, especially in a freezing snap or when one side of the greenhouse is exposed to a prevailing cold wind. These heaters, which work entirely through convection, will be far more useful if they can be fitted to fans or, even better, to a network of perforated polyethylene tubes to push the air out evenly. Whatever your choice, do not hesitate to seek the advice of a heating expert.

When selecting pipes to carry hot water, decide on the 1½-in. diameter, rather than the old 4-in. system. Although you will need a greater length of the small-bore pipe, and it will cool down quickly, it will save you money, because there is much less water to heat. In addition, the small pipe will give you much better control over the greenhouse temperature, as it responds quickly to the demands of the thermostat. (In longer greenhouses, 2-in. pipe may be needed to give good water circulation over the entire length.)

With the 1½-in. pipe, there may be some problems when it comes to water circulation, so budget for a circulating pump. If the difference in temperature between the water in the pipes and the air in the greenhouse is 100° F., the amount of heat given off by them, per foot, will be:

DIAMETER (in.)	HEAT EMITTED (Btu to nearest round figures)
1	80
1¼	100
1½	110
2	130
2½	150
3	190
3½	200
4	230

To figure out how much piping you will need, divide the figure above into the total heat load for the greenhouse, which you worked out before.

Armed with all the economic arguments about various heating systems, you can now go ahead and choose the one that suits you best for price and convenience. On the whole, pipe systems, whatever the heating method, are the most economical to run, but much depends on the cost of the fuel, and they are more expensive to install. The cheapest sort of oil burner — rather than oil stove — is a vaporizing one, which is installed in a steel or cast-iron jacket. Rely on expert installation if you choose this system. Unless the flame and the draft are carefully regulated, much of the gas produced will be wasted.

Always put the boiler on the side of the greenhouse that is sheltered from the prevailing winds. This will stop flue gases from staining the glass. If you can, put the boiler outside the house, on the north side — it will work more efficiently, be protected from the wind, and emit a steadier draft.

The advice of a heating engineer or horticulturalist is a must before installng a pipe system. The final layout will depend on the pipe diameter you choose and on whether you add a pump to assist the circulation. In general, pipes work best on the so-called *thermo-syphon principle*. The pipes rise one inch in every ten feet, and at the highest point in the system there is a tank or valve. The temperature in the pipes is kept constant because hot water rises, is cooled, and falls to the bottom of the system. A drainage point — fixed on the boiler or return pipe — is vital. From it, the pipes can be drained when not in use during cold weather, to prevent cracking, a procedure which is *all important*.

Modern circulating pumps largely do away with the need for a thermo-syphon system, which means that pipe layouts can be much more flexible. Pipes can be put where they fit most conveniently, and flexible rubber couplings can be used instead of metal ones. They can be used under benches for propagation, then dropped to ground level when the benches are removed to plant, for example, a crop of tomatoes. This particular versatility is especially useful for providing heat for warmth-loving crops.

TYPE OF SYSTEM	AVERAGE OPERATIONAL EFFICIENCY (%)	APPROX. RUNNING COSTS PER 100,000 Btu's (therm) at fuel prices as stated
Solid-fuel boiler, simple design. Hard coal.	50	Based on coal at 12,000 Btu per lb. Cost of fuel per cwt. 90c = 15c 72c = 12c 60c = 10c 48c = 8c
More refined solid-fuel boiler using smokeless fuel or coke.	60 70	Based on value of 12,000 Btu/lb. Cost of fuel per cwt. 90c = 12½c 72c = 10c 54c = 7½c $1.00 = 12c 84c = 10c 68c = 8c
Oil-fired boiler and fan heaters with external fuel (Some types have no flue, and this results in slightly higher operational efficiency.)	75	Based on oil at 130,000 Btu per gallon. Cost of fuel per gal. 25c = 25c 20c = 20c 15c = 15c 10c = 10c
Gas-fired boiler	75-80	Base the cost on price of gas per therm, which varies from area to area, but deduct 20 to 25% for loss of efficiency
All types of electrical heaters (Residual heat from storage heaters is considerable and is difficult to allow for in comparative tables. Off-peak rates are sometimes lower than those stated here, but cannot be computed.	100	(Consult Power Company for variable rates.) Cost per kwh 5c = $1.45 4c = $1.16 3c = 87c 2c = 58c 1c = 29c

Tubular heaters are one of the most reliable and economic ways of heating a greenhouse. *Courtesy of Humex.*

Control is simplicity itself if you have an electrically operated system, for it can be linked up to a thermostat which gives a high degree of control. Constant attention, however, is the only secret of success with a simple oil-fired stove. Solid-fuel boilers, too, need much care if they are to keep the greenhouse temperature even, but today's gas and oil pipe systems are self-regulating from a thermostat within the greenhouse. Any pipe system that is thermo-syphoned, however, whether heated by soild fuel or by oil, will be demanding on effort, but these can be made easier to control if fitted, respectively, with a thermostatic flue regulator or a thermostatic control that automatically lights or extinguishes the flame. A pipe system that depends exclusively on a circulating pump can be controlled through a thermosat linked to the pump itself, rather than to the boiler. This means that the boiler can be left to reach its own temperature and is constantly poised to supply heat, but it is dangerous if pipes are made of cast iron, for these may be damaged by sudden expansion. An electrically operated valve will have much the same sort of controlling effect.

In a porch or conservatory it is tempting to install off-peak storage heaters that run off the domestic supply, but these may not be very efficient. A simple on/off heater will, for example, produce too much heat on a warm day following a cold night. Even with a storage heater that has a controllable input and output, you

An aluminum lean-to greenhouse with direct access to the dwelling house. Such greenhouses are easily heated from the domestic heating system.

may need to fit proper ventilators to regulate the temperature effectively. Another alternative is to heat your porch or conservatory with narrow hot-water pipes from the household supply, but control will again be a problem if your time switch is set to halt the heater overnight. Better still, keep the boiler temperature constant. Link one time-control clock to the circulating pump of the domestic supply, and fit a separate pump to the conservatory system. If the conservatory system is self-contained, it can be regulated with temperature-sensitive valves within the pipes. Hot-air heating will present you with very similar problems, so always take the trouble to seek expert help.

Ventilation and shading

Controlling the heat of a greenhouse is closely linked with other environmental problems, especially those of ventilation and shade. Because warm air is lighter than cold air, it rises, and if this air escapes through ventilators, then heat, and also humidity, can be controlled with ease. The best place for vents is usually — although not always — the highest point of the greenhouse. As the hot air escapes, cold air is drawn in through the vents, either by simple exhange or under the pressure of the wind. It also comes in through glass overlaps, gaps under the door, and any other poor fittings.

The rate at which air change takes place depends mainly on the size and position of the ventilators. Ventilators placed down low, through which cool air will rush in, can speed up the air change enormously. If possible, make sure that the total ventiltor area is at least a fifth of the floor area, calculated with the vents wide open, although, in fact, many small greenhouses are poorly supplied with ventilation, and you may have to settle for less than the perfect situation.

Ventilating fans are first rate for greenhouse ventilation, with the proviso that they change the air 50 to 60 times per hour and that they do not create so much air movement as to damage plants or slow their growth. The best fans, therefore, are large ones, with slow rotations, with a shutter so that air will not enter when the fan

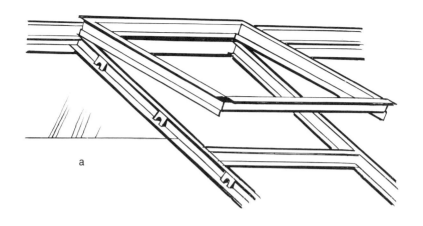

a

Two different types of ventilator.
(a) The fan-light type. (b) The louver type.

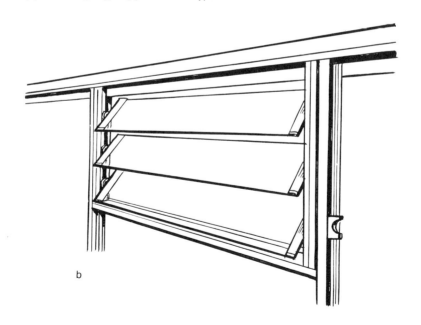

b

is not working. Make sure there is a good air inlet opposite the fan. For even greater control, you can install the fan with a time switch or, better, with a thermostat.

The latest method of ventilating a greenhouse is that of air conditioning. Cool outside air is pushed into the house and escapes through leaks in its superstructure, through plastic vents that open when the air pressure reaches a certain level. When the humidity drops, the air is moistened by an automatically controlled humidifier, and heaters may also be linked into the system. A time clock is useful for adapting the fans to run off and on at intervals throughout summer nights and thus prevent an excessive build-up of condensation.

Conventional ventilators are easily adapted to fit into an air-conditioning system. Electrical attachments will ensure that the vents open when the greenhouse reaches a certain temperature, by pulling them open by a cable or by operating "winder." Less expensive are ventilator "lifts" that react to rises in temperature by expanding and lifting clear of the ventilator, thus letting cold air in. So, apart from a few ventilators that you would open by hand in very hot weather, your entire greenhouse air condition can be remote-controlled.

For many pot plants, for successful early propagation, and for treating tomatoes suffering from attack by *Verticillium* wilt, the best way of reducing the heat in the greenhouse is by shading. Blinds — either the venetian or roller kind — are effective, particularly if they are green, and they can be fixed either inside or outside the greenhouse. Although it gives you less flexibility, painting the outside of the glass with a mixture of lime and water, plus a little size, is equally effective, as the whiteness reflects rather than absorbs sunlight. Or you can buy a green-colored shading compound, but both will wash off over the summer months, and any coloring still in place in October can be brushed off, so that plants get as much light as possible during the winter months.

The desert rose *Adenium obesum,* a curious, succulent plant with a huge, swollen base and brilliantly colored flowers.

Left A propagating unit control. This is easily adjusted by removing the small rubber protective cap and turning the dial with a screwdriver. *Courtesy of Humex.*
Right A simple greenhouse thermostat heating control unit. A unit of this type is relatively inexpensive. *Courtesy of Humex.*

2 Basic Equipment

Benches and shelves — Watering — Soil-warming — Propagation units — Lighting

Benches and shelves

Benches and shelves are a useful addition to any greenhouse, and when planned with imagination, they will give you not only storage space but also much more room for all sorts of activities. Slatted benches made of lengths of pressure-treated wood measuring 4 x ¾ in. and fitted into iron or galvanized steel fitments are ideal for housing pot plants, boxes of seedlings, and for propagation done in boxes or pots, for warm air will filter easily between the slats. Solid benches made of wood or asbestos transite are best filled with rooting mediums for raising cuttings or used for mist propagation (see p. 48). Like slatted benches, they are best constructed at table height — 30 to 34 in. — and made 3 to 3½ ft. wide.

Some gardeners think that solid benches should be used exclusively for pot plants, and there is some sense in this argument, but whatever you decide on, always make sure that there is an air space between the bench and the greenhouse wall so that warm air can percolate upward.

Shelves fixed high up are very useful for keeping plants near the light during the winter months, or you can have two tiers of

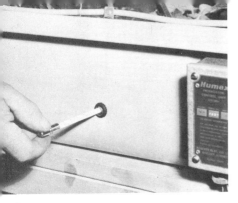

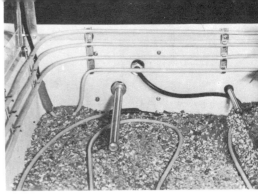

Propagating unit controls. The temperature in the sand can be checked by withdrawing the special thermometer. *Courtesy of Humex.*

The inside of a propagating case, showing the air-warming cables attached around the sides of the case. *Courtesy of Humex.*

benches. Use the upper tier for propagation, seedlings, and so on, and the lower tier for storing less-hardy plants over the winter.

Watering

Your greenhouse watering equipment need be nothing more than a watering can and a cold-water tap, but you may want to follow the lead of commercial greenhouse gardeners and install an automatic or semi-automatic watering system. Water is sprayed onto plants from above or at soil level, or it reaches pot plants through individual tubes. Controlled electronically, the water can have soluble nutrients added, through a fertilizer injector that is fitted between the tap and the hose outlet, which literally "waters down" the chemicals. For some plants it is important that the water applied by 55° F. or warmer, but not over 90° F.

Rather than fitting a completely automatic system, many amateur gardeners prefer to water their greenhouses with a fine mist from a special pipe called a spray line. These spray lines are easy to fit into a small greenhouse and will work well as long as the pressure and volume of the water is high enough. Electrically operated valves can be attached to the system, and these inexpensive devices mean that you can direct water onto your plants at the flick of a switch.

Ceramic blocks can be fitted into the greenhouse water supply.

The Humex "Tricklematic" fully automatic watering system. Such systems are a far more reliable way of supplying plants regularly with the right amount of water than haphazard can-watering. *Courtesy of Humex.*

These control the amount of water being released, as water rapidly evaporates from their porous surfaces. When choosing watering cans for the house, select those with long spouts and fine roses, in either metal or plastic.

If you decide to specialize in growing pot plants, it might be well worth considering a capillary watering system, although you can use one for other growing projects, too. In principle, a completely level solid bench is lined with polyethlene to make a completely watertight basin 3 or 4 in. deep, and a perforated pipe is placed to run down the center of the bench. The basin is then filled with sharp sand which will draw up the water.

The pipe for the capillary bench is best placed inside some drainage tiles or sections of curved asbestos, as this will help prevent the holes in the pipe from becoming blocked. By attaching the bottom end of the pipe to a fish tank fitted with a ball cock it is easy to keep a steady water level between ½ in. and 1 in. below the surface of the sand. Or you can operate a capillary setup with a slow-running hose or possibly special drip nozzles which, as their name suggests, drip water constantly onto the sand. For the greatest possible sophistication, the water input can be electronically controlled.

Placed on top of the sand in the bench, pot plants will absorb water by capillary action: the sucking power is produced by the plant roots and by the water-attracting properties of the sand. As long as you do not make them too strong, solutions of mineral nutrients can be added to the bench. Choose plastic rather than clay pots. They will work more efficiently.

Soil-warming

The soil in your greenhouse benches can be adapted to grow heat-loving plants simply by warming it, or you can get good results by warming the benches or pots themselves. Provided the growing medium is warm, many plants will grow well in cool air. The growing medium — soil, bench, or pot — can be kept warm very inexpensively. The warming process is particularly effective if used *before* planting those plants that thrive on heat. For while the soild quickly heats up if warmed directly, the same process takes a long time, and is much more costly, if only the air in the greenhouse is warmed by pipes that do not touch the growing substrate. Another advantage of soil-warming is in propagation. Often, you will want to heat a small amount of soil or compost to a high temperature in order to assist rapid rooting.. If so, a soil-warming system will prove invaluable.

The method of soil-warming is quite uncomplicated: electric lead-covered cable is laid 1 to 2 in. deep and 3 to 9 in. apart in sand under potted plants or at the bottom of the propagating bed.

There are three way of controlling your soil-warming equipment. The most popular is the dosage method, in which the heating element is turned on for a fixed period every day or every night, where electricity is obtainable at a cheap, off-peak rate. The temperature of the soil will fall very little while the heating is turned off. Although 8 or 10 hours of heating in every 24 will probably be enough, you can link the system to a time switch.

The second heating method is via a thermostat embedded horizontally in the soil. Unnecessary for most amateur operations, this control system is particularly well suited to growing plants that constantly demand high temperatures. Thirdly, you can simply insert a thermometer into the soil and turn the electricity on or off as you think best. If in doubt, you can be sure of good advice from your power company, from a qualified electrician, or from equipment suppliers.

Propagation units

Success in propagation will depend almost entirely on your ability to induce cuttings of stems or leaves to make roots, and thus become self-supporting, as quickly as possible. The greatest problem is to keep the stem healthy all the while, for viable roots are unlikely to form if, aboveground, soft leaf tissue is in the process of wilting. In a propagation case, the temperature and humidity of the air are higher than normal. The loss of moisture from the leaves — called transpiration — is thus cut down to a minimum. The tissues of stem and leaf stay full of water and stiff, making propagation much easier and root formation more rapid.

The most humble sort of propagating case is a polyethylene bag. Placed over a box or pot, it will efficiently retain both heat and moisture. A sheet of glass over a box will have the same effect. More-complex propagating cases consist of a solid bench, which can be filled with the growing medium and which is heated, covered by a "frame" made of glass or polyethylene. In addition,

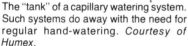

The "tank" of a capillary watering system. Such systems do away with the need for regular hand-watering. *Courtesy of Humex.*

A moisture meter. Such meters are the most accurate method yet devised of deciding when a plant needs watering. *Courtesy of Humex.*

the case can be fully lit and the whole carefully controlled by means of a thermostat, quite independently of the temperature and humidity of the greenhouse itself.

One disadvantage of propagating cases is that they may get too hot and damage the plants. To avoid this, you could consider installing a mist propagation unit, using water warmed to 70 to 75° F., which heats the soil to a constant temperature while, at the same time, spraying the cuttings with a fine mist of water from spray nozzles.

Lighting

Although you may want to light your greenhouse to change the length of the day or to increase the light intensity in fall and winter, the main use of lighting is to make working in the greenhouse possible in winter and during the evenings. Make sure that you fix

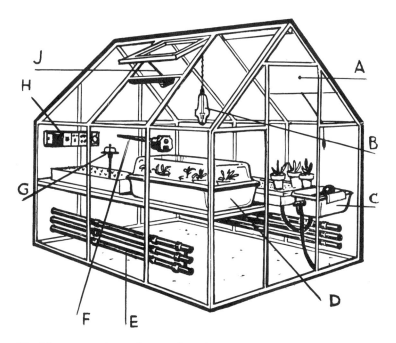

The fully automated greenhouse: all you have to do is watch the plants grow. (A) Shading blinds on spring rollers: these can be controlled by a photo-electric cell. (B) An electric fumigator. (C) Header tank for automatic capillary-action watering system. (D) Propagator case with soil-heating cables, and automatic temperature control. (E) Automatic tubular heaters controlled by, (F) rod-type thermostat. (G) Mist propagation unit. (H) Control panel. (J) Automatically operated ventilator.

the lights in positions that do not cast too much shadow and where you do not have to constantly duck to avoid them. This will throw out light to best advantage all over the greenhouse. You can add extra bulbs to light benches or dark corners that you use frequently in winter. Be sure to choose waterproof light fittings.

3 Caring for Greenhouse Plants

The greenhouse environment — Plant nutrients — The basic ingredients of artificial media — Artificial media — Mixing the artificial media

The greenhouse environment

Because a greenhouse can overcome the changeability of the weather, it will not only support exotic blooms in their natural state but also plants that the breeder has tailored to fruit or flower at convenient times. Although not entirely successful, plant-breeding has resulted in a vast range of plants in which the best qualities of different species and varieties are blended to give the best of quality, color, disease resistance, fruit production, and so on.

The really important thing about a greenhouse is that although it supports plants having growth cycles essentially similar from seed or cutting to mature plant, these plants are often far from their natural habitats and so need special care. Tropical plants are not, for example, merely tender and sensitive to frost. Tomatoes, whose original home was sunny South America, need, despite intense breeding, all the light they can get, especially during the winter. Plants from the world's tropical forests require the hot, humid, shady environment typical of their home. And ·a lot of perfectly hardy plants find their way into the greenhouse because they will grow there at an unusual season of the year. Lettuce, for example, is supremely successful outdoors in a cool summer but will thrive during the winter in a heated greenhouse.

The artificial conditions of the greenhouse call for thoroughness and patience when growing plants. Inside the house there are light and air but no moisture unless you supply it. The sun shines in summer, and there is an excessive build-up of heat, which has to be remedied. In winter, when there is less sunshine, you have to produce a substitute. In these warm, often humid conditions, plants grow much more quickly and so need more water and more plant food than those growing outside.

Another important side effect of the greenhouse atmosphere is the tremendous difference between the conditions during day and night. This is especially so in spring and fall, when warm, sunny days are often followed by cold nights. The result is a huge temperature variation, which can result in reduced growth.

One of the great advantages of the greenhouse over the outside is that whereas outdoors the results of your efforts will be, after a few years, quite unpredictable, in the greenhouse you can control and predict plant behavior with considerable accuracy. To get the most from your greenhouse, take advantage of these special features. Compared with the garden, you can start with soil or media that is free from pests and diseases, and with physical properties that are precisely what you want them to be. You start with no weeds; none will arrive unless you introduce them; and you can add or subtract heat, light, and nutrients at will. Do not take chances with doubtful seeds or soil, composts, or cuttings. The same factors of total environmental control that enable the plants in the greenhouse to thrive will also enable weeds, pests, and diseases to flourish if they once get a hold.

The first essentials for plant growth are, as we have seen, light, air, and water, plus heat, either to trigger growth or to induce a cutting to produce roots. The demand for these conditions increases as the plant grows. How much the demand increases is governed to a large extent by how large the plant becomes, by the weather, and by the time of year. Plants also need minerals, which

Coleus are among the most colorful of greenhouse plants grown wholly for their foliage. When raised from seed, a vast variety of color forms can be expected.

are mostly absorbed from the soil via the roots and transported, within the plant, to the sites of growth, flower, or fruit production. To help the greenhouse gardener balance the mineral needs of the plants in his care, fertilizers, and liquid feeds are available in vast numbers. It is as well to know something about what they contan and what the plant will need before you begin any dosage, either to the soil or directly to leaves and stems, for plants can absorb nutrients from these parts as well as from the roots.

52

Plant nutrients

Different species may require variations in plant food supply, and a seedling may not need the same diet as a mature plant. What is most important is a proper *balance* of nutrients, for just as the human frame needs proteins, carbohydrates, fats, and vitamins, in varying amounts, so plants need a mixture of minerals such as nitrogen, potassium, and phosphorus.

Another reason for keeping a constant check on the balance of plant nutrients is that plants grow more quickly in the greenhouse than they do outdoors. Their requirements therefore change more rapidly. Make sure, then, that the plant nutrients are well maintained throughout the growing period.

The sort of plants that will grow well in any soil depends to a large extent on the acidity or alkalinity of the soil. The substance that has the greatest effect on this important quality is limestone. In chemical terms, limestone is calcium carbonate, which is an alkali. Plants need limestone, and the calcium carbonate also helps to keep the soil sweet by neutralizing the soil acids.

Chemists record acidity or alkalinity as a number known as the pH value. A lime-rich soil will have a pH of about 8, while an acid-rich soil such as peat will have a pH of around 4. The ideal pH for the greenhouse varies from plant to plant, but many will thrive in pure peat or a mixture of peat and sand. Unlike the peat of natural bogland, greenhouse peat preparations contain few microorganisms, so that little acid is produced, and the environment remains stable. A soil of pH 6.0 to 6.5 is generally useful for greenhouse plants.

Four chemical elements are essential for the health of all plants:

Nitrogen. Plants absorb nitrogen from the soil in the form of chemical compounds called nitrates. Nitrogen is needed for the development of the leaves and probably for all plant growth. However, any plant will suffer if you give it either too much or too little nitrogen. An excess of nitrogen, particularly an excess in relation to the amount of potassium the plant is getting, will lead to large, fleshy leaves and small flowers and fruits. When nitrogen is in short supply, the reverse happens. The leaves are small and flowers and fruits are of normal size. The color of the leaves is a good guide to the amount of nitrogen being supplied. Pale green or yellow leaves indicate too little nitrogen; a very dark green indicates too much.

Phosphorus. Found in the soil in chemical combinations called phosphates, phosphorus is essential to plants because it is involved in the growth and development of roots, stems, leaves, and flowers. Without phosphorus, plants cannot use the carbohydrates they build up in photosynthesis and cannot manufacture new cells. Good root production and early maturity are both impossible without phosphorus, but an excess or deficiency of this element is very difficult to pinpoint just by looking at a plant. The best guide to phosphorus shortage, however, is a dark-green or bluish tinge on the leaves.

Potassium. The role of potassium in the life of plants is a complex one. It is important in root development and in water transport, and it contributes to making plants more disease-resistent. Potassium is vital to the formation of fruits and seeds and to the manufacture of chlorophyll. Give plants potassium in the form of potassium sulfate or as potassium nitrate. The leaves will give you clues to the dosage. Too much potassium results in hard, dark leaves; too little results in flabby, pale-green growth. Experience will be your best guide, but remember that many crops, especially tomatoes, absorb nitrogen and potassium together. Give too much of one, and the plant will not be able to take in the other, so take the trouble to balance each one.

Magnesium.   Magnesium is involved in the vital process of photosynthesis. Some crops, including tomatoes, have large demands for magnesium, but the element is absorbed along with potassium, and both elements are needed for proper magnesium uptake.

The basic ingredients of artificial media

Good feeding in the greenhouse will be enhanced if you put plant roots in high-quality soil or some other growing medium. While ordinary garden soil may be enriched with compost or "humus" formed from the breakdown of leaves and other garden refuse, some gardeners use the word compost to mean specially prepared mixtures, enriched with nutrients, which form an excellent environment for the roots of greenhouse plants. We elect to call these mixtures "artificial media."

Artificial media are mixtures of various substances, of which the most important are as follows:

Loam. Ideally, loam is the end-product of the partial rotting of sod from a grass pasture 4 to 5 in. thick, stacked grass-downward for about 6 months. Depending on the soil and the quality of the grass, loam can vary enormously. Really reliable loam is, in fact, difficult to obtain, but a good substitute is the top 9 to 12 in. of the soil, although this will be low in organic matter and variable in mineral supply. If using the "second-best" loam, always avoid soil that you know has been infested with diseases and nematodes, and choose material with particles that are neither too coarse, like sand, or too fine, like clay. Check the acidity of the loam, and sterilize it.

Peat. A greenhouse gardener can choose from many different kinds of peat, but the ideal peat for composts is light in color and open in texture. Avoid dark, fine peats or those with a black, decomposed look, or use them sparingly with fibrous peat to step up its mineral content. If in doubt, wet the peat and press out the water. The darker it is, the less desirable is the peat.

Good-quality peat acts like a sponge and so helps the growing medium to store both wate and minerals. At the same time it allows air to get to the plant roots. A high-quality peat, supplied in a polyethylene bag to keep it moist, can be guaranteed to be free of pests and disease-carrying microorganisms. Peat is most valuable to plants in the long rather than the short term. The minerals it contains cannot be used immediately, but over a matter of months peat encourages growth of microorganisms that, in turn, make the nutrients available.

Leaf mold. Once used very widely in compost-making, leaf mold has recently fallen from favor because its quality is too variable. Despite this, you can make good use of a well-matured leaf mold from a mixture of leaves of deciduous trees. Compost

The flourishing array of plants is being grown on a gravel tray watered by a capillary watering system. Water trickles through the gravel, and the plants take up just sufficient water for their needs. *Courtesy of Humex.*

containing leaf mold is particularly good for growing tomatoes and chrysanthemums, which demand nourishment over a long period.

Sand. Whatever its particle size, small amounts of sand will give a compost body and porosity. Always select sand that is neither acid nor alkaline. Make sure that it is free from contamination and, preferably, intermediate in texture.

Vermiculite or perlite. These two substances, made respectively of expanded mica and of volcanic ash, are valuable additions to compost, as they can absorb large amounts of water. Although their names may be unfamiliar, neither is a new comer to the horticultural scene, and they can be bought from reputable suppliers.

The most popular primrose of all, *Primula malacoides* — the perfect plant to raise in the greenhouse for use as a house plant.

Artificial Media

Several substitutes for soil have been developed in recent years. These usually contain varying proportions of sphagnum peat moss, perlite, vermiculite, pine bark, and/or sawdust. Combinations of these materials give a lightweight mix that is generally disease-free and, with proper nutrients and a favorable environment, will produce good plant growth. If more weight is desired in the mix, clean, sharp sand may be added.

Some of the many possible formulations are listed here. No single formulation has been found to be best for all greenhouse crops. Quantities given in each case will make two bushels of mix.

Modified U. C. Mix Research at the University of California and grower experience in that state have led to the development of this mix:

1 bushel fine, clean sand
1 bushel sphagnum peat moss
2 ounces potassium nitrate
4 ounces 20% superphosphate
10 ounces ground dolomitic limestone
6 ounces calcium carbonate limestone
2/3 ounce iron sulfate

Cornell Peat-lite Mix A. This mix is basically a combination of sphagnum peat moss and vermiculite in equal volumes, to which nutrients are added in sufficient quantity to provide for suitable plant growth. One of these formulations is as follows:

1 bushel sphagnum peat moss
1 bushel No. 2 or No. 4 horticultural vermiculite
7 ounces calcium sulfate
1 pound ground dolomitic limestone
2 ounces potassium nitrate
4 ounces 20% superphosphate
½ teaspoon Sequestrene 138 iron chelate
1½ teaspoon Fritted trace element 503

Cornell Peat-lite Mix B is essentially the same as Mix A, except that horticultural grade perlite is substituted for the vermiculite.

Pine-bark mixes. Plant-growing media containing pine bark have proved satisfactory for many kinds of greenhouse-grown bedding plants as well as for production of greenhouse tomatoes, cucumbers, and other greenhouse vegetables. One of the several possible combinations is made as follows:

1 bushel No. 2 or No. 4 horticultural vermiculite
1 bushel screened pine bark
1 pound ground dolomitic limestone
7 ounces 8-24-8 commercial grade fertilizer
1 ounce potassium nitrate
1½ ounces water-soluble trace element mix (such as Peters S.T.E.M.)
1½ ounces wetting agent (such as ''Aqua-gro'')

In this greenhouse advantage has been taken of the greenhouse border, of inter-mediate staging, and high-level staging. Ferns or ground-cover plants could also be grown under the staging on the right.

Mixing the artificial media

The best place to mix small volumes of media is on a concrete floor. A small concrete mixer can usually be rented for mixing larger volumes. The simplest way to apply the small amounts of trace elements and wetting agent is to mix them in water and work it uniformly into the media while mixing. Each batch should be mixed for at least five minutes to assure uniform distribution of the nutrients. These mixes may be stored if kept in plastic bags and not allowed to become dry.

Slow-release fertilizers such as Osmocote 14-14-14 may be added to these mixes. Good results have been obtained from the Cornell Peat-lite Mix A and the pine-bark mixes by adding 12 ounces of Osmocote 14-14-14 to each two bushels at the time of mixing. This is in addition to the other ingredients indicated.

Rather than assembling all of the ingredients required for the

Staked tomatoes outdoors. Plants were started in the greenhouse to hasten fruiting.

formulation of the mixes given, you may prefer to utilize one of the several commercial plant-growing mixes available. These are already mixed, with fertilizers, minor elements, and all necessary ingredients incorporated, ready to use. Some of the mixes available under brand names include ''Pro-Mix,'' ''Jiffy Mix,'' ''Redi-Earth,'' and ''Kys-Mix.''

When you use any artificial soil media, be sure to use clean pots, flats, or other containers to avoid contamination of the media with disease-causing organisms.

If the media is stored outdoors in cold weather, bring it into the greenhouse and let it warm up before using it.

Tomatoes are a popular greenhouse crop. Here they are grown by the strawbale method commonly used in England.

4 Pot Plants

Pot plant needs — Flowering plants

Though still far from rivaling the Dutch in the number and excellence of their pot plants, home greenhouse gardeners are fast realizing the pleasures of cultivating these members of the indoor team. With a little persistence plus plenty of common sense you can produce a whole galaxy of color and variety. Your greenhouse will not only provide you with the absorbing interest of pot plants, but will mean plants in your home all year.

Pot plant needs

Pot plants vary enormously in their habits and grow and flower at different times throughout the year. The secret of success is knowing when the plants need water and nutrients, controlling the environment carefully, selecting the right compost, and putting it in a pot that is neither too big nor too small. Except for cacti and slow-growing pot plants like ferns, most actively growing pot plants will need a liquid feed every 10 to 14 days. Although you may be far from 100 percent successful, especially at the start, do persevere with pot plants in the greenhouse, With experience, you will find them a most rewarding hobby.

As far as equipment is concerned, for growing pot plants you need a well-situated, properly ventilated greenhouse, free from drips. It should have a good, clean water supply and a heating system that can keep the temperature at about 50 to 55° F. Inside the greenhouse you will need a fairly extensive layout of benches. A tiered setup will not only create more space but will make your display look more attractive. Keep a convenient corner of a bench, either in the greenhouse or in a nearby shed, for potting. You may also get good use from a storage area to house ingredients for soil mixtures, although this is far from essential now that reliably formulated mixtures can be easily obtained. Make sure you have enough room for storing pots and flats, and bear in mind the possibility of fixing a permanent propagating case, although you can easily make do with a temporary "rooting bench" for a few years.

The way you start off your pot plants will depend on the individual species. Some are perfectly successful when started from seed, while others are best propagated from cuttings, which you may have to obtain from friends or neighbors, either as cuttings themselves or in the form of stock plants. Plan your planting carefully, so that each plant is in the right place at the right time of year, and be sure to use the correct soil mixture.

Flowering plants

The range of pot plants that will thrive in a greenhouse is enormous, but begin with only a few simple sorts. Primula, pelargonium, coleus, fuchsia and many annuals make excellent pot plants and are relatively simple to grow. Many cacti are simplicity itself, but tuberous begonia, cineraria or streptocarpus can be a little more difficult.

Annuals in pots. Some of the best annuals to grow in pots inside the greenhouse, to give both color and cut flowers, are:

Acrolinum	Larkspur
Antirrhinum (technically a perennial)	Nasturtium
Arctotis	Nemesia
Calendula	Petunia
Felicia	Ursinia
Godetia	Zinnia

Sow the seeds in March or April, and pot out the seedlings in 3-in. pots. Then simply supply them with moderate heat.

Orchids. At present there is much interest in orchid-growing, but it need not be the exclusive province of the professional. Many orchids merely need a cool rather than hot greenhouse, but all demand humidity and shade in summer. The basic medium for orchid-growing is equal parts of sphagnum moss and fiber from the osmunda fern. Add some broken crocks to give good drainage. Rather than risk disappointment, it is well worth taking the time to consult a book devoted to orchid-growing, and you can also join one of the orchid societies.

None of the following orchids is difficult.

For the cool greenhouse

Coelogyne	Oncidium
Cymbidium	Odontoglossum
Dendrobium	Paphiopedilum (some)

For the warm greenhouse

xBrassolaeliocattleya	xLaeliocattleya
Cattleya	Paphiopedilums

For the hot greenhouse

Phalaenopsis	Vanda

Alpines. Andromeda, *Campanula garganica,* Cassiope, Crocus (winter-flowering), Cyclamen, Cytisus, Dianthus, Dodecatheon, Draba, *Dryas octopetala,* dwarf conifers, Helleborus, Hepatica, Lewisia, Narcissus (dwarf types), Primula, Rhodohypoxis, Saxifraga, Sedum, Sempervivum.

A cool greenhouse is an excellent place to grow alpine plants. These natives of the world's mountain ranges will make your greenhouse both colorful and interesting. Like orchid-growing, this is rather specialized, and you will gain much from becoming a member of an Alpine society or rock-garden club.

As well as specific pot plants, many shrubs and herbaceous plants will bloom much earlier in the year if potted and cultivated in the greenhouse. The list of plants is virtually endless.

Pleomele reflexa, a delightfully variegated but very slow-growing greenhouse shrub. Needs good light to color well.

Vines and shrubs. Many tender vines and shrubs are ideal occupants for a lean-to greenhouse. Choose, for a start, from any of these:

Bougainvillea   *Jasminum*
Cobaea scandens   *Plumbago capensis*
Ipomea rubro-caerulea

Ferns. You can grow any number of ferns in a greenhouse. They do particularly well on a north-facing side, which is shady and moist. Some ferns that should thrive are:

Adiantum cuneatum   *Pteris cretica albolineata*
Adiantum decorum   *Pteris cretica major*
Adiantum elegans   *Pteris tremula*
Cyrtomium falcatum   *Pteris wimsetti*
  (Holly fern)

Ferns can be propagated in several ways. Many can be successfully grown from spores, but the fern *Asplenium bulbiferum* can be multiplied from small, bulb-like structures called bulbils. Other ferns throw out runners from which new plants can be cultivated. A fern easily propagated in this way is *Nephrolepis,* in which miniature plants are produced at the ends of the runners. These will grow independently if merely pegged down into the earth, where they will root.

65

Greenhouse Pot Plants (Flowering Plants)

SPECIES	VARIETY	EASE OF CULTURE*	PROPAGATION	FLOWERING TIME	AVERAGE HEIGHT	TEMP REQ.†	NOTES
ACHIMENES	Various colors	T	Rhizomes (tubers) Mar./Apr.	May-Sept.	6-9 in.	I	Dry out rhizomes over winter
APHELANDRA	Squarrosa louisae	T	Cuttings, various times. Use propagation case	Various	12-16 in.	H	Can be difficult to grow and needs steady temperature.
AZALEA	Indica	D	Cuttings in spring in propagation case	Xmas on	12-16 in.	C/I	Grafted plants can be retained for years.
BEGONIA	Semperflorens	E	Seed Feb. on	June-Sept.	6-12 in.	I	Tubers rest in winter
	Tuberous (double)	E	Start tubers Feb.	June-Sept.	12-15 in.	I	
	Gloire de Lorraine	E	Cuttings mid-Aug. Cuttings Feb. on	Nov.-Feb.	9-12 in.	I	
BELOPERONE	Guttata (Shrimp Plant)	D	Cuttings in Apr. in propagating case	Summer	12-16 in.	I	Needs a little shade in summer. Give plenty of water
CACTI	Various types	E/T	Various methods. Sections of stems, etc. also seed	Various	Various	C/I	Dozens of different types. Most can be grown in frost-free greenhouse. Give plenty of sun.
CALCEOLARA	Herbeohybrida (Hybrida multiflora)	T	Seed in July/Aug.	Mar.-May	12-16 in.	C	Cool, steady growth. Put in 5- to 6-in. pots for flowering
	Multiflora nana	T					
CAMELLIA	Japonica	D	Leaf-bud Cuttings Mar. Pot in 6-in. pots	Winter/ early spring	18-24 in.	C	Line-free compost essential. Stand in cold frame in summer
CAMPANULA	Isophylla alba	E	Cuttings in Mar.	Summer	Pendulous	C	Ideal for hanging baskets or edge of staging
CAPSICUM (grown for decorative fruit)	Annuum	T	Seed in Feb.	Fall on	10-12 in.	C	Keep cool. Shade if necessary. Spray frequently when flowering to assist fruit formation
CELOSIA	Argentea cristata Pyramidalis	E	Seed in Feb.	May-Sept.	15 in.	C	A fairly simple plant to grow for garden. Gives good color and lots of interest

*Key D = Difficult; E = Easy; T = Tricky.

† C = Cool; I = Intermediate; H = Hot.

Name	Variety	Type	Propagation	Season	Size	Temp	Notes
CINERARIA	Grandiflora, multiflora, multiflora nana	T	Seed May/June	Spring on	12-15 in.	C	Place outside in summer in shaded position. Keep cool in greenhouse not above 55° F.
CRASSULA	Rochea coccinea	E	Cuttings in spring	June on	9-10 in.	C	Add lime to compost. Cold frames in summer
CYCLAMEN	Persicum	D	Seed space sown Sept.-Jan. Pot early and keep corm above soil level. Corms can be potted in Aug.	Aug. on	9-10 in.	C	Flowers in 5- to 6-in. pot. Cold frame or cool greenhouse in summer. Regular feeding essential
ESCHEVARIA	Retusa	E	Sections of stem with rosette of leaves after flowering	Winter	9-10 in.	C/I	A relatively easy plant to grow. but dislikes overwatering
ERICA (Heath)	Gracilis, gracilis alba, nivalis, hyemalis, willmorei	T	Tip of stem cuttings, ¾ in. long, in Nov./Jan. Root in 3 parts peat, 1 part sand in propagating case	Throughout winter	12-18 in.	C	Lime-free compost. Stop frequently to encourage bushy growth. Takes 2 years to develop. Plant outside during second season
FUCHSIA	Fulgens (many different varieties)	E	Internodal cuttings Jan./Feb. in individual containers. Root in propagating case	Summer/fall	Various	C	Frequent feeding essential. Give plenty of air and water in later stages of growth. Stake. Bad for white fly
GENISTA	Cytisus canariensis	E	Cuttings Jan./Apr. Takes 2 years to produce good plant	Spring	12-24 in.	C	Really a shrub. Merely requires cool growing and regular trimming to keep bushy. Stand outside and keep shaded during second season. Lift in for winter

				Flowering period	Height	Temp.	Notes
GERANIUM	Zonal Pelargonium. Regal Pelargonium. Many lovely varieties; the new Irene strain has prolific blooms. Ivy-leaved, especially for hanging baskets. Scented, variegated	E	Cuttings at various times of year. Fall or spring. Individual containers or open propagating bench	Long flowering period	Various	C	One of the easiest plants to grow. Do not overwater; keep feeding
GLOXINIA		T	Seed in Jan./Feb. Tubers, leaf cuttings mid-April in propagating case	Aug./Sept.	9-12 in.	I	Needs constant watering and feeding
HIPPEASTRUM	Amaryllis	T	Pot bulb in 5- to 6 in. pot for starting in spring. Dec. or earlier	Xmas/spring	18-20 in.	I	
HYDRANGEA	Macrophylla (many excellent varieties)	D	Internodal stem cuttings Feb./May (non-flowering shoots only). Trim leaves to reduce transpiration loss	Spring	16-20 in. or taller	C/I	Stand outside in summer, or in cold frame. Pinch plant to encourage leaf growth. Keep nitrogen and phosphate levels low during feeding. Use iron sequestrine if foliage turns white.
IMPATIENS	Sultanii (Busy Lizzie)	E	Seed Feb./Mar. or cuttings at various times	Summer	10-15 in.	C/I	A very simple plant to grow. Must have plenty of light
MARGUERITE	Crysanthemum frutescens (white), C. coronarium (yellow)	E	Cuttings Aug./Jan. Seed Feb.	Summer	12-16 in.	C	Keep cool. Stop frequently to induce bushy plant
POINSETTIA	Euphorbia pulcherrima	D	Stem cuttings July to Sept.	Winter	2-4 ft.	C/I	Avoid dryness. Grown for colored bracts
POLYANTHUS	Primula polyanthus	E	Seed in May. Pot into 3½-in. pots	Early spring on	9-12 in.	C	In frame during summer. Keep cool and well watered. Lift into greenhouse Dec.

			Propagation	Flowering	Height	Temp.	Notes
PRIMULA	Malacoides kewemsii sineusis	E	Seed sown thickly May-June. Pot into 5-in. pot	Spring/summer	9-12 in.	C	Avoid overwatering in winter. Apply iron sequestrine if yellowing of foliage occurs.
ROSES	Dwarf types	T	Buy and pot in 8-in. pots Oct./Nov. and cut back hard	Summer	16-18 in.	C/I	The object is merely to advance flowering. Use any good compost and keep feeding.
SAINTPAULIA	lionantha	T	Seed in spring (do not come true from seed). Leaf cuttings. Shade from direct light	Flower over a long period	6-9 in.	I/H	Feed regularly with high potash feed. Keep well watered and warm
SALPIGLOSIS		T	Seed in Sept.	May	2-3 ft.	C	Grow cool
SALVIA	Blaze of Fire, Harbinger	E	Seed in Jan./Feb. Flowers in 5-in. pot	Summer	9-12 in.	C	Really a bedding plant, but excellent in pots. Keep cool in summer
SCHIZANTHUS	Poor Man's Orchid	T	Seed Aug.	Apr./May	12-24 in.	C	Grow cool. Give plenty of light and adequate support. Pinch out to ensure bushy growth
SOLANUM	Capsicastrum, pseudocapsicum (attractive fruits)	D	Seed in Feb. Cuttings Feb. in propagating case	Winter, especially Xmas	12-16 in.	I	In shady frames in summer, lifting out during Sept. Stop plant height to induce bushy growth. Syringe frequently during flowering to induce setting. Save seed of good forms
STOCKS	Beauty of Nice	E	Seed July/Aug.	Spring		C	Keep cool and airy
STREPTOCARPUS		T	Seed Jan./Mar. Leaf cuttings in Aug.	Aug./Oct.		C	Feed and water regularly
ZANTEDESCHIA	Aethiopica (Calla)	T	Division in July/Aug.	Easter on	2-3 ft.	C/I	Rest outdoors in summer before repotting
ZYGOCACTUS	Truncatus (Xmas Cactus) syn-epiphyllum	E	Sections of stem segments in spring	Xmas on	pendulous	C	Keep in cool in summer. Give plenty of water. Repot occasionally

Greenhouse Pot Plants (Foliage Plants)

SPECIES	VARIETY	PROPAGATION	HEIGHT	TEMP.	NOTES
ARALIA (Fatsia)	Fastsia japonica	Root cuttings in Mar.	2-3 ft.	C	Green, healthy, fig-like leaves
BEGONIA	Rex (many other types)	Leaf or stem cuttings anytime in propagating case	12-24 in. and taller	I	Water sparingly in winter
CHLOROPHYTUM	Comosum variegatum (Spider Plant)	Layer small plantlets to ground	12-18 in.	C	Easy plant to grow
CISSUS (Grape Ivy)	Rhomboidea	Leaf-bud or heeled cuttings in propagating case	12-24 in.	I	Needs support
CISSUS (Kangaroo Vine)	Antartica, striata	Leaf-bud or terminal cuttings	12-18 in.	I	An excellent foliage plant. Keep well supported
COLEUS	Blumei (many varieties and color forms)	Seed-variable colors. Cuttings rooted in propagating case in spring.	1-2 ft.	I	Must have plenty of light. Keep well watered
CROTON	Codiaeum variegatum	Cuttings with at least 6-7 leaves. Also leaf-bud cuttings. Both in propagating case	1-2 ft.	I	Give full light and keep cool. Shade only in full sun
DIEFFENBACHIA	Picta (Dumb Cane)	Terminal and stem cuttings, the latter with 2 buds horizontally. Both in propagating case	1-2 ft.	I	A fairly easy plant to grow
DRACAENA	Inc. Cordyline	Stem cuttings. Cordyline australis and C. terminalis from seed Feb./Mar.	18 in.	I	Shade and high humidity necessary
FATSHEDERA	A cross between Fatsia japonica and Hedera helix	Terminal and leaf-bud cuttings in propagating case	18-24 in.	I	Must be well supported
FICUS	Elastica decora, lyrata (Fiddle-Leaf Fig) pumila	Leeaf-bud and terminal cuttings in propagating case	1-2 ft.	I/H	Avoid cold temperature
GREVILLEA	Robusta (Silk Oak)	Seed Nov./Mar.	2 ft.	I	Cool and shade required
HEDERA	The Ivies	Tips or leaf cuttings any time	Trailing	I	Easy to grow. Ideal for edge of staging

MARANTA	Leuconeura kerchoviana	Division of roots in spring			
PEPEROMIA	Angyreia (sandersii) hederifolia	Leaf-bud cuttings or leaf-blade sections	1-2 ft.	I	Easily grown
			9-12 in.	I	Easy to cultivate
	Obtisifolia "variegata"	Leaf-bud or terminal-stem cuttings. All in propagating case			
PHILODENDRON	Various species which include a number of related plants such as Scindapsus aureus and Montstera deliciosa	Leaf-bud cutings in propagating case or terminal-stem cuttings	12-16 in.	I	Needs support, shade from sun
PILEA	Cadeiri	Nodal or terminal cuttings in propagating case	9-12 in.	I	An easy plant to grow
SANSEVIERIA	Trifasciata (Bowstring Hemp)	Cuttings from leaf tip or suckers (variegated types)	16-18 in.	I	An indestructible plant. Easy to grow
SAXIFRAGA	Sarmentosa (Mother-of-Thousands)	Runners, root separating, or from seed		C	One of the easiest plants to grow
SELAGINELLA	Many different types	Cuttings	4-6 in.	I	A useful plant for shady greenhouse
TRADESCANTIA	Various varieties including Zebrina — Wandering Sailor	Cuttings	Trailing	I	Easily grown plant with variegated leaves. Ideal for edge of bench

5 Bulb Forcing

**Choosing and planting bulbs — daffodil — tulip
— crocus — gladiolus — hyacinth — iris —
freesia**

Although it need not be done in a greenhouse, bulb forcing is a hobby that offers any gardener plenty of scope for producing showy flowers in large numbers well before outdoor bulbs have burst into bloom. Bulbs are easy to deal with and need little or no artificial heat. Select well-known, reliable suppliers. High-class bulbs cost little more than poor-quality specimens, yet the extra money is a good insurance against disappointment.

Choosing and planting bulbs

The bulbs that will flower the earliest are usually specially treated by the growers and can be bought ready-planted in bowls of fiber or can be planted in soil in boxes or pots in your own greenhouse, with the tip of the bulb just showing. Pot hyacinths, tulips, and daffodils in October.

Because rooting is quickest and most prolific at low temperatures, put the planted bulbs in a cold frame or a sheltered corner of the garden or cellar, and insulate them with a covering of moist peat or sand. They are unlikely to need watering, but if the weather is very dry, give the covering an occasional, but thorough watering.

Once the growing shoots are green and have pushed well aboveground, so that 1½ to 2 in. are showing, lift the bulbs into a warm greenhouse — it should be between 55 and 60° F. At first keep tulips and hyacinths in the dark and daffodils in the light. After 7 to 10 days, when the flower stems are well lengthened, give them more heat and full light, either in the greenhouse or in your house. Later-flowering bulbs can, however, be brought straight into the light, but, whichever method you choose, always make sure that the soil does not dry out.

Many bulbs, particularly tulips and daffodils, do well if planted in deep boxes. There they will give you cut flowers early in the year. For pot-planted bulbs, an alternative to bringing them out from darkness to daylight is to force them to flower in artificial light at a temperature of 65 to 70° F. A warm cellar is ideal for the purpose. For every square yard of space you will need one 100-watt light bulb. Switch these lights on for 12 hours in every 24. The greatest disadvantage of forcing bulbs in artificial light is that they tend, especially daffodils, to sprout too many leaves and not enough flowers.

Daffodil. One of the largest and least troublesome of plants, the daffodil or narcissus offers a greenhouse gardener an enormous choice. For the earliest flowers, choose well-established varieites like "Paper White" and Grand Monarch. For later on, the Barnie, King Alfred, and Trumpet groups are probably the gems of the whole family.

Pot up daffodils and narcissi in a rich compost of ¾ leaf mold and ¼ peat moss. Keep them insulated in peat or sand in the dark, until the spears of the leaves look green and you can feel the flower bud clear of the neck of the bulb; then give them constant light and air. By November the early flowers will need some warmth, while the rest will appreciate a rise in temperature from December until March. Avoid intense heat until the bud is fully out of the bulb. Always stake daffodils and narcissi well to keep them from bending and breaking.

FOR CHRISTMAS. "Paper White," "Grand Soleil d'or."

JANUARY ONWARD. "Barrie," "King Alfred," "Mrs. R. O. Blackhouse," "February Gold," "Cheerfulness," "Silver

Chimes," "Polar Ice."

Tulip. In myriad varieties, growing in number year by year, tulips will flower in pots from Christmas until the end of May. For old-established favorites, choose Prince of Austria and General de Wet to bloom earlier, followed by Mendel, Triumph, and finally Darwins. Pot your early varieties in September or October in a loamy soil and the later ones can wait until November.

Force your early tulips by keeping them in the dark. As soon as the flower buds appear, they can have constant light. The later sorts will probably not need the dark and will develop naturally with very little heat.

Crocus. Most members of the crocus family flower early and if planted in good time — in September or October — will bloom in January or February, or even at Christmas. After planting, cover the pots with peat or sand for five weeks, then keep them in a cold frame until December or January, when you can bring them into the warmth. Try to avoid sharp temperature changes, especially from cold to hot. That will make the foliage grow long and spindly, and the blooms may fail.

EARLY. "Brilliant Star" (scarlet), "Prince of Austria" (orange-scarlet), "Sunburst" (yellow).

EARLY DOUBLE. "Dante" (blood red), "Electra" (cherry-red), "Mr. Van der Hoef" (rich yellow).

EARLY DARWINS. "Kansas" (white), "Glory of Noord-wijk" (rose-pink), "Elmus" (red edged white).

COTTAGE. "Dreaming Maid" (white edged violet), "Marshall Haig" (scarlet, yellow center), "Palestrina" (pink inside, green outside).

Gladiolus. This beautiful plant will flower much earlier in the greenhouse than outdoors, but you cannot force it as hard as tulips or daffodils. For the best results, put them in a greenhouse bed filled with a rich loam, 6 in. apart and 3 in. below the soil surface, in February or March. Or put the largest ones in 6- to 8 in. pots.

Hyacinth. With a little forethought, you should be able to have these heady-scented flowers in bloom for Christmas. Pot Roman hyacinths in late August or early September, and keep them under a sand pile for about 5 weeks. By November you should be able to bring them into a slightly warmed greenhouse in full light. Following Roman hyacinths, plant other varieties to give a good show right through until April.

BLUE. "King of the Blues" (deep blue), "Ostara" (deep blue, very early), Lilac "Amethyst" (violet).

PINK AND RED. "Gipsy Queen" (tangerine), "jan Bos" (bright red), "Pink Pearl" (deep pink), "Scarlet Perfection" (double scarlet).

WHITE. "Carnegie" (pure white), "L'Innocence" (pure white, large bells).

YELLOW. "Prins Hendrik" (clear yellow), "Yellow Hammer" (golden yellow, early).

MINATURES. "Vanguard" (light blue, early.)

Iris. Like gladioli, bulbous irises can be planted in the spring, but there are many varieties that will give you color in the months of March and April if planted in the fall. Do not force these irises, but plant them in borders or pots in the greenhouse and leave them to develop naturally in their sheltered environment. Set them about 3 in. deep and 3 to 4 in. apart. The varieties Wedgewood and Imperator are best for fall planting.

Freesia. Many people count freesias as their favorite flowers — their scent is delicious and their blooms are bright but delicate. Thanks to modern plant breeding, freesias come in a wonderful range of colors. You can grow freesias either from seed or from corms. Sow seed in April; plant the corms in August or September.

Freesia corms thrive in a loamy soil and need plenty of ventilation. Until growth starts, cover the pots with an inch of moss, but remove it as soon as the leaves start to show, so that they can grow unhindered. At this stage, they can be taken into the greenhouse, but do not let them get too hot — a place near the glass is ideal.

There are three main methods of growing freesias from seed. Firstly, the seeds can be sown in boxes of moist peat, covered with a sheet of glass and paper, and kept at a temperature of 55 to 60° F. Once the germination process is complete, the seedlings can be pricked off, 2 in. apart, into 9-in. clay pots filled with loamy soil

Hibiscus rosa-sinensis, the greenhouse hibiscus. This has far larger and more colorful flowers than the hardier *H. syriacus,* which can be grown outdoors.

plus peat. Secondly, the seeds can be sown direct in the containers, but in this case germination does tend to be erratic. Thirdly, you can sow the seeds individually into peat blocks, which can then be planted in pots or in greenhouse beds, but this method takes up a lot of greenhouse space, and the foliage is far more prolific than the flowers.

During the summer months take the young plants, in boxes or pots, out into a cold frame. Fed and watered regularly, they should make good growth. In September, take the plants back to the greenhouse. With water and moderate warmth they will soon flower and will give you many weeks of color. Help prevent the plants from flopping and breaking by staking them.

Another color form of *Hibiscus rosa-sinensis*. This one has flowers over 8 in. across. Breeding in tropical countries is extending the range of color and size of flower.

6 Raising Summer Bedding Plants

Plants in the greenhouse — Propagation

Although many gardeners buy summer bedding plants from their local nurseries, there is much more satisfaction in growing your own plants, either from cuttings or from seed. As well as a sense of achievement, you will be able to grow just the colors and varieties you want. The greenhouse is exactly the right place to give these plants a good start in life.

Plants in the greenhouse

Dahlias and begonias are summer bedding plants that need special care, as neither will tolerate the slightest frost. Start by bedding the respective corms or tubers in moist peat during February and March and giving plenty of warmth. Conventional cuttings can then be taken and rooted normally. Or you can store the tubers and corms in a frost-free place over the winter and plant them out or pot them in late April or early May, when they should grow naturally.

After they have overwintered in a frost-free greenhouse, many plants such as *Centaurea* or *Salvia* can be divided in spring. Use a sharp knife to split the plants; then pot them in separate pots.

The easiest and most common way to raise bedding plants is direct from seed. You will have to plant these seeds at different times, as some take longer than others to develop. For good measure, sow one seed pan of each species you select. As they grow, prick the seedlings off into boxes or containers with many separate compartments. Watch out for damping off — once it starts it will spread through a while batch of seedlings very rapidly, and there is little you can do to stop it. This is particularly common in lobelias and antirrhinums. For this reason, choose a soil-free growing medium such as peat and perlite or peat and vermiculite.

The whole spectrum of bedding plants contains, as you might expect, some perennials, some annuals, some hardy, others half-hardy or tender. For convenience, all can be given the same kind of treatment. Your aim should be to have them ready to set out in the garden as soon as the spring displays are over, probably in mid-May, although the exact time will vary from region to region and possibly from year to year. In northern areas, or if plants are very tender, be patient and wait until late May before you expose your carefully tented greenhouse plants to the rigors of the weather.

Propagation

Although you will want to synchronize your timing, different bedding plants will need different treatments. Seeds are easy and should present few problems, but taking cuttings can be more tricky. These cuttings can be taken either from hardy or half-hardy perennials in September to October or from the same plants before they are lifted out of their summer beds. Another alternative is to take cuttings in the spring from plants that have been overwintered in a frost-free greenhouse, although some are tolerant of freezing temperatures.

Clip off sturdy cuttings 3 or 4 in. long and, preferably, although not necessarily, without flowers. Trim them, and place them 2 in. apart in boxes containing a rooting medium of sand and peat or either alone. A frost-free greenhouse will now come into its own,

Dwarf marigolds are one of the many annuals that can be started in the greenhouse for bedding out later in the season.

for although the cuttings may survive, root, and grow in a sheltered cold frame or with a sack draped over them, the greenhouse will prevent massive losses of cuttings as the result of frost, snow, and damp.

Do not struggle or be impatient for quick growth. Large plants produced too soon will be a nuisance rather than an asset. In the same way you can take your time with cuttings from plants that have been overwintered in the greenhouse. In this case you can encourage the cuttings to root more quickly by keeping them in a warm place, either in boxes or on a warm propagating bench. During the early part of the year, once strong growth begins, take the cuttings out of the greenhouse and put them into good soil in a cold frame or, if they are exceptionally hardy, like pentstemons or geraniums, into individual 4-in. pots. For geraniums use a potting soil of equal parts of loam, sand, and peat. To make for strong growth, put them into a place in the greenhouse that gets a good light.

Plants for summer bedding

NAME	PROPAGATION	COLOR	HEIGHT	DIST. APART
AGERATUM	Seed in February/March	Blue	4-9 in.	6 in.
ALYSSUM	Seed in February/March	White, pink	4-6 in.	6 in.
ANTIRRHINUM	Seed in February/March	Various	12-18 in.	10-12 in.
ASTER	Seed in March	Various	12-18 in.	10-12 in.

80

NAME	PROPAGATION	COLOR	HEIGHT	DIST. APART
BEGONIA (Fibrous rooted)	Sow seed or take cuttings of overwintered plants in spring	Various	9-12 in. and higher	9-12 in.
BEGONIA (Tuberous)	By division of tubers after start of growth in spring or by seed in February/March	Various	9-12 in. or more	9-12 in.
CALCEOLARIA	By cuttings in fall or spring	Red and yellow	12-15 in.	9 in.
CARNATION (Marguerite or Chabaud)	Seed by spring. Alternatively by cuttings or by layering during previous summer	Various	12-14 in.	12 in.
DAHLIA	Seeding in spring for dwarf bedding types, or cuttings from overwintered tubers when growth starts. Tubers may also be planted	Various	1-6 ft.	1-3 ft. (bedding types at 1 ft. apart)
DIANTHUS	Seed in February	Various	12-15 in.	10-12 in.
FUCHSIA	Cuttings taken in fall to spring	Red, pink, purple	18 in.-3 ft.	18 in.-3 ft.
GERANIUM (Zonal Pelargonum)	From cuttings taken in spring or fall	Pink, white, red	9-12 in. (also trailing types)	9-12 in.
GLADIOLUS	By corms planted direct or started in heat prior to planting outside in May	Vast range of colors	1½-3 ft. or more	6-12 in.
HELIOTROPE	By cuttings taken in spring	Blue	9 in.-3 ft.	1-3ft.
LOBELIA	Cuttings may be taken in spring. but seed is usually sown in February	Blue, white, pink	6-9 in.	6-9 in.
MARIGOLD (French & African)	Seed sown by February/March	Orange shades	9 in.-2½ ft.	12-15 in.
MESEMBRYAN-THEMUM	From cuttings or by seed sown in spring	Various	Trailing	9-12 in.
MIMULUS	Seed in February/March	Yellows	12-15 in.	10-12 in.
NEMESIA	Seed in February/March	Various	9-12 in.	12 in.
NICOTIANA	Seed in February/March	Shades of white, pink, etc.	12-18 in.	12 in.
PENTSTEMON	By cuttings taken in spring or fall	Various	1-2 ft.	12 in.
PETUNIA	Seed in February/March	Various	12-15 in.	12 in.
PHLOX (drummondii)	Seed in spring	Various	12-15 in.	10-12 in.
SALVIA patens	By division cuttings in spring	Blue	1½-2 ft.	10-12 in.
SALVIA (Scarlet)	Preferably by seed in February, but also by cuttings	Scarlet	1-2 ft.	9 in.
TAGETES	Seed in February/March	Orange/Yellow	10-12 in.	9-12 in.
VERBENA	Cuttings in spring or by seed in January/February	Various	Trailing	12 in.

7 Chrysanthemums and Carnations

The needs of chrysanthemums — Chrysanthemum types — The growth of cuttings — Propagation — Greenhouse chrysanthemums — Carnations

For producing flowers in fall and winter, chrysanthemums are absolutely unbeatable and deserve a place in every greenhouse. Even the most inexperienced greenhouse gardeners will enjoy growing chrysanthemums, and his living-room can be full of color until Christmas.

The needs of chrysanthemums

Although chrysanthemums can be grown outdoors, the greenhouse is essential if you want blooms after the winter frosts have set in. Rather than plant seeds, the best way to grow chrysanthemums is from cuttings, and, while these will survive in a cold frame, the greenhouse offers a much more risk-free environment.

Chrysanthemums are interesting plants because, except for some early varieties, they will only form flower buds when the days are short. So, unless there are less than 14½ hours of daylight in every 24, you will get no buds or blooms. Botanically, chrysanthemums are perennials, and the part belowground, the rootstock, is hardy and resistant. Flowers and foliage, too, can stand fairly low temperatures, but much depends on type and variety. Although chrysanthemums can only be grown outdoors in the months between spring and fall, in a greenhouse they will flourish all year, but without shading they will naturally flower only in the weeks when the days are short.

Chrysanthemum types

Because there are so many chrysanthemum cultivars, and because new ones are constantly appearing, it is difficult to be specific about the best sorts to grow. Rather, find a good catalog from a specialist chrysanthemum grower and make your own choice of sizes and color schemes. Visit flower shows, local and national, to get an idea of what is going on, or join a chrysanthemum society to hear the latest in cultivars and growing methods.

From all the variety of shape and form, experts often divide chrysanthemums into several different types:

Incurved. In these chrysanthemums, all the petals turn inward to make a ball-shaped flower.

Incurving. The Petals of these flowers are much looser and do not form a tight ball.

Reflexing. In these flowers, the petals droop or turn outward.

Singles Rather than a conventional flower with many rows of petals, singles have a central eye surrounded by a single ring of petals.

Anemone-flowering. These chrysanthemums are like singles, but the central eye is raised like an anemone.

Spider or Japanese. These types have tubular petals and may be either the standard or pompon types.

Pompon or Spray. These have a few too many flowers per stem in a branched-stem arrangement. The flowers vary from small 1 in. or less, fully double button kinds to large ones, 2½ to 3 in. in diameter, and may be single, semi-double, double, anemone, or spider-flower types.

Large exhibition chrysanthemums have immense flowers. They can be incurved, incurving, or reflexed. Other chrysanthemums have varying blooms and can flower early, mid-year, or late. They have one flower pen stem and are called standards.

If you try to economize when buying stock, you may be disappointed, so spend the extra money on ensuring good quality. Throughout the year keep an eye on the plants and quell any disease as soon as it appears. Plan your chrysanthemum show from year to year. The best time to choose stock for taking cuttings is when the plants are in full flower, but do not hesitate to reject any plants that have the slightest sign of distorted flowers, weak growth, or mottled leaves.

To grow chrysanthemums in the greenhouse, you will need to keep the temperature at a minimum of 45 or 50° F. to get fall and winter flowers. Good light is a must, and you will need a bench — either slatted or solid, with a capillary watering system — if you plan to grow chrysanthemums in pots. To harden off your cuttings a frame is a good idea, but it is not essential.

The growth of cuttings

As they grow, your chrysanthemum cuttings will produce several shoots, but you can manipulate the plant to produce the kind of flowers you want. If you want several large, single blooms on each plant, completely remove the tops of the single stems when 6 to 9 in. of growth has been achieved and the buds are beginning to break. Done carefully, without bruising the plant, this will encourage side shoots to grow. After this, you can take off all but the central bud on each side shoot. This is known as disbudding.

The only chrysanthemums that do not need disbudding are the spray varieties, which, when untampered with, produce enormous numbers of small, starry blossoms. One word of warning: do not top chrysanthemums at the same time you are moving them. This is too much of a shock. Instead, wait until the plants are well established in their new positions.

There are three main methods of chrysanthemum-growing, each with its own advantages, but the one you select will probably depend on the cultivars you choose.

Chrysanthemums are very popular as greenhouse plants. Above is one of the smaller growing Charm chrysanthemums, which can be grown from a cutting taken in May or June to a full-size plant covered in flowers by fall. Below is one of the large-flowered hybrids.

Pots. In this method, chrysanthemum cuttings are first rooted in boxes, then transferred to 3-in. pots, and then into 8- or 9-in. pots, in which they mature and flower. Use a fertile, well-drained mixture such as equal parts of sand-loam soil and peat.

To stop the larger plants from keeling over, put three or four strong canes, each about 4 ft. long, around the edge of each pot, and tie twine between them. For a few days put the pots in a square to give them plenty of natural protection; then arrange them in a line along the greenhouse wall at 6-in. intervals. Give regular water and liquid feed, and turn the pots from time to time to make sure each plant gets even light and so the roots do not grow out of the pot and into the ground below.

Lifting. In the lifting process, the chrysanthemum cuttings are first established in pots and then lifted into beds inside the greenhouse. The best time for this lifting operation is September or early October, well before the winter frosts set in. At this stage, you will probably have the young plants in 5- or 9-in. pots (for details see the previous section) or growing in good, rich soil outdoors in a sheltered spot such as a cold frame.

For good results, it is worth the trouble of preparing the greenhouse thoroughly before putting the chrysanthemums inside. Fork over the soil in the beds, an add 4 to 6 oz. of a good general fertilizer to every square yard. Using a shovel, and keeping as much soil as possible around the roots of each plant, lift the chrysanthemums into the bed. Water them well. You may notice some wilting over the next few days but the plants will recover quickly as long as you keep the greenhouse cool. After a couple of weeks, heat the greenhouse to the 45 to 50° F. mark.

Direct planting. Although a great favorite with commercial chrysanthemum growers, direct planting is often a nuisance for amateurs because it takes up so much greenhouse space. This, in turn, means that if you choose the direct-planting method, you will only be able to have one other crop before them. Because they develop much more quickly in the greenhouse, there is no need to put in chrysanthemum plants until well into the summer. Choose your time, from mid-June to mid-August.

Another difficulty of direct planting is that it may be difficult to grow or obtain cuttings that are at the right stage of maturity. One good idea is to take cuttings early in the year, establish them in the greenhouse, and stop them when they are growing vigorously by pinching out the tops; then take another set of cuttings and root those.

Chrysanthemums planted direct will do best if kept at a constant temperature of 55 to 60° F., especially when the buds are forming in September and October, and, of course, regularly fed and watered. When feeding them, concentrate particularly on nitrogen and potassium, and make sure the greenhouse is well ventilated. Support the plants well, and allow plenty of pace — a maximum of 10 in. — between each.

Propagation

Plan your propagation program well in advance, so that you are ready to take cuttings at the right time of year. Take cuttings of large, exhibition greenhouse chrysanthemums in March of late-flowering and those that bloom in the middle of the season in March or April, and of early-flowering chrysanthemums in April and May.

Select your cuttings from plants that have been overwintered in a protected frame or frost-free greenhouse. From below a joint, take each cutting 2 to 3 in. long and about ⅛ in. in diamter. Always strip off the lower leaves, then dip the cuttings in hormone powder. For rooting, make up a mixture of equal amounts of peat and sand, and put in the cuttings ½ to ¾ in. deep and 1 to 1½ in. apart in flats. Water them well, then keep them at 55 to 60° F. Within 14 to 21 days the cuttings should have rooted (you can tell when rooting is well established because the tips of the cuttings become a fresh green) but you can help speed the process by covering the box with a sheet of plastic to keep in air and moisture or by using a proper propagating unit. One particularly good way of propagating chrysanthemums is to put the cuttings into peat blocks, and this method is well worth considering.

Once cuttings have rooted, transfer them to 3-in. pots filled with a loam organic matter mixture or some other good compost. Or you can plant them, 5 in. apart, in a good, rich soil in a cold frame.

There are several hundred chrysanthemum cultivars on the market for both greenhouse and garden use. The following are widely grown and are adapted for greenhouse culture.

Standards. "Albatross," white. "Blaze," red with bronze reverse. "Dark Orchid Queen," lavender-pink. "Detroit News," medium bronze. "Escapade," light pink. "Fred Shoesmith," white. "Good News," yellow. "Indianapolis Yellow," light golden-yellow. "Princess Anne," pink. "Sunburst Mefo," golden yellow. "Yellow Mefo," light yellow.

Pompons. "Alabaster," white. "Beauregard," orange-bronze. "Bluechip," lavender. "Goldcap," golden yellow. "Iceberg," white. "Icecap," white. "Jack Straw," yellow. "Rusticon," rust red. "Sunbeam," golden yellow. "Telstar," shell pink. "Yellow Polaris," lemon-yellow.

Spiders. "Maple Leaves," bronze. "Silver Strand," white. "Streamer," lavender-pink. "Tokyo," white. "Yellow Tokyo," yellow.

Carnations

As long as your greenhouse is light, airy, and can be heated to 50° F. or more, it should be an excellent spot for growing carnations.

Buy young carnation plants early in the year, and arrange for them to be delivered in April. At this stage, they will be in 3-in. pots ready for moving into 6-in. pots with No. 3 John Innes compost or for planting out in beds. These beds should consist of soil raised 8 or 10 in., supported with concrete at the sides, and should have drainage holes at the base.

When the plants are well established, take off the tips to encourage side shoots to grow. Once these side shoots are 5 or 6 in. long, they too can be topped so that each bears a single bud. Regular watering is a must for carnations, as well as an even temperature of 55 to 60° F. Always avoid abrupt changes of temperature, which will damage the plants, and give them plenty of air. As the carnations get taller, you will need to support them with canes.

As soon as you have cut your first carnations, you can begin feeding with a complete fertilizer. To keep a regular supply of stock going, take cuttings in early and late spring. This will also mean that you have a good supply of plants to replace old ones that are becoming "leggy" and that you can ward off rusts and the red spider, which are the carnation's worst enemies. For cuttings, choose shoots well above the base of the plant and just below the flowers. Root them in sand.

There are many cultivars of carnations to select from, but a majority of those now being grown in greenhouses are kinds that have sprouted from or are related to the cv. "William Sim," a red. These include "Light Pink Sim"; "Linda," pink; "Red Gayety"; "Scania," red; "Shocking Pink," salmon-pink; "Tangerine," orange; "White Sim"; "Yellow Sim"; and variegated types such as "Mamie" or "S. Arthur Sim," both white and red.

8 Vegetables

Heating and ventilating for vegetables — Beds — Tomato — Cucumber — Lettuce — Root crops — Snap beans — Other forcing crops

In a properly heated and ventilated greenhouse it is possible to produce many kinds of vegetables during the fall, winter, and spring months when it is not possible to grow these crops in the outdoor garden.

Since greenhouse space is more costly to maintain than outdoor gardening space, only those vegetables that produce relatively high yields in a small space and those that will produce under low light intensity and short-day conditions should be considered.

The use of supplemental light to compensate for short days may be considered. If used, provide at least 20 watts of lighting per square foot of area lighted. This may be provided by using fluorescent lights with the tubes spaced six in. center to center. Fixtures should be adjustable so the lights are at least 12 in. above the plants being lighted. They can be controlled manually or by a time clock to provide for a total day length of 14 to 16 hours. One of the main disadvantages of providing supplemental light is that during daylight hours the fixtures shade the plants. Of course, this problem could be solved if the lights could be moved each day from directly over the plants, but this would be more trouble than most greenhouse owners would care to tolerate.

Vegetables grown in the home greenhouse include tomato, cucumber, lettuce, radish, onion, carrot, pepper, and eggplant. All these crops should be grown from seeding to maturity in one of the artificial media such as UC mix, Cornell peat-lite mix, or pine-bark mix, previously described.

Heating and ventilating for vegetables

Greenhouse temperature control is more of a problem where several kinds of vegetables are grown in the same greenhouse. Crops such as lettuce, carrots, radishes, and onions will grow well enough with a minimum temperature of 40 to 50° F. Tomatoes, however, should not be grown at temperatures below 60° F., and cucumbers do best if the minimum temperature is 70° F.

If all kinds of vegetables are to be grown in the same greenhouse, some sort of compromise is necessary. The best is probably to set your heating thermostat to call for heat when the air temperature is 60° F. at the level of the plants. If more heat is needed for cucumbers, heating cables may be installed on top of or buried several inches deep in the medium. If electric heating cables are used, make sure they are installed according to the manufacturer's instructions and that a thermostat is used to prevent the temperature of the artificial medium from exceeding 85 to 90° F.

The best way to ventilate the greenhouse is to use exhaust fans operated by a thermostat or to use automatic vent openers. These should be activated by a thermostat, centrally located in a shaded place in the greenhouse. For most greenhouse vegetables, the ventilating thermostat may be set at 70 or 75° F. during winter months, and 75 or 80° F. during the summer.

Beds

The beds in which greenhouse vegetables are grown should be constructed of weather-resistant materials such as redwood, cypress, or other wood treated with a non-toxic preservative. However, do not make the beds of any wood that has been treated with creosote or pentachlorophenol. Several "salt" preservative treatments are satisfactory, and lumber treated with one of these is usually available locally.

Bed dimensions will vary, depending on the size and arrangement of benches, walks, etc., in the greenhouse. Beds in which artificial media are to be used should be 6 in. deep and lined with plastic. For single rows of plants such as tomatoes or cucmbers, they may be as narrow as 12 in., or for double rows, 30 to 42 in. Plants set in double rows should be "staggered"; that is, set in an alternate or zigzag pattern.

Tall-growing crops, such as cucumbers and tomatoes, should be on the north side of the greenhouse or along one end where they will not shade low-growing crops. Where it is possible, rows should run north-south to provide more uniform light distribution during the winter months.

Tomato

This is probably the most popular of greenhouse vegetables. Almost every person who wants a greenhouse envisions being able to harvest a bountiful supply of red-ripe tomatoes during midwinter. By following standard production practices (and with a bit of luck), this may be possible.

A typical production program would be as follows:

Cultivar. "Floradel," "Manapal," "Michigan-Ohio Hybrid," "Tuckcross D," "Tuckcross M," or "Tuckcross 520." For small-fruited types, the red cherry tomato may be grown. It is very vigorous and sets fruit freely under adverse weather conditions.

Seeding dates. It may be more practical to consider growing a spring crop and a fall crop rather than try to carry a fall crop through the winter, since tomatoes set and develop fruit poorly during the short days of midwinter. For the two-crop system, the fall crop should be seeded between June 15 and June 30 and the spring crop between December 15 and January 1. As soon as the seedlings are 1 in. high, transplant to 3- or 4-inch peat pots; transplant to the beds 3 to 4 inches later, before any flowers are open. Set the plants about 18 to 30 in. apart in the row in any pattern to provide 4 to 5 sq. ft. bed space per plant. For the average family, 6 to 8 plants should provide enough tomatoes for home use.

Culture If the plants are grown in one of the artificial media such as Cornell peat-lite or pine-bark mix, it will be necessary to supplement the plant food in the mix as the plants develop fruit. This may be done by adding water-soluble fertilizer every sixth or seventh watering at the rate of 1 oz. per gal. per 4 plants. When the days are longer and temperatures higher, more frequent watering and feeding will be required than under short days when growth is slow. Supplemental feedding should not begin before fruit begins to set on the second cluster.

Another means of providing supplemental feeding is to apply Osmocote 14-14-14 (three-month formulation) at the rate of 6 oz. per plant, distributed evenly over the surface of the growing medium. This should be adequate for most of the production period.

Regardless of the fertilizer program used, additional trace elements will need to be added to the medium every 8 to 10 weeks. One way of doing this is to use Peters S.T.E.M. (soluble trace element mix) at the rate of 1 tablespoonful per gal. of water, applied to 6 plants. Do not wet the foliage with this solution.

As the plants grow, it will be necessary to train them to a string, stake, or some other support. Break out all side shoots that develop in the leaf axils along the main stem, before they get to be 4 in. long. As the fruit begins to ripen, the lower leaves may turn yellow and begin to die. These should be removed by breaking them off the main stem. To help prevent development of botrytis and virus diseases, all plant pruning of shoots and leaves should be done by breaking them off rather than cutting them from the plant. If a knife is used and one plant is infected with a virus disease, the healthy

A collection of vegetables, many of which are started in the greenhouse for earlier production.

plants could be infected with the virus from the knife blade. If leaves are cut off, leaving a short stub at the main stem, botrytis could readily infect the entire plant through the piece of leaf left attached to the main stem.

To obtain adequate fruit set on greenhouse tomatoes, it is necessary to mechanically dislodge the pollen, which subsequently settles on the stigma of the flower, thus achieving pollination. This is easily accomplished by using a battery-operated vibrator daily on each flower cluster so long as flowers are open on the cluster.

Disease and insect control may be problems at times. One of the best ways to prevent diseases from being a problem is to do everything possible to discourage their development. Some of these practices include:

1. Maintain at least 60° F. minimum temperature.
2. Remove all plant prunings from the greenhouse.
3. Provide adequate ventilation.
4. Use recommended fungicides regularly.
5. Do not wet foliage of plants when watering.
6. If possible, grow your own plants.
7. Control insects such as aphids, which transmit diseases.
8. Keep the relative humidity below 90%.

Cucumber

Cucumbers may be grown in the same greenhouse as tomatoes, although cucumbers do best if the minimum temperature is 70 instead of 60° F., as required for tomatoes. The best type to grow is the parthenocarpic type, so-called because they are seedless and do not require pollination for development. In fact, they should not be pollinated, or low-quality fruit will develop.

There are several cultivars of these so-called "European" or "English"-type forcing cucumber. Some of the newer cultivars produce only female flowers, reducing the chance of pollination. Of course, if cucumbers are growing outside at the same time of year, it is possible for pollen to be brought into the greenhouse by bees, resulting in pollination of the greenhouse cucumber.

The production schedule for cucumbers should be similar to that practiced for tomatoes, with a fall crop being harvested from early fall until midwinter and a spring crop being harvested from March until outside-grown cucumbers come into production. The fall crop should be seeded between August 1 and September 1 and the spring crop between January 1 and February 1.

Plant one seed each in 2¼-in. peat pots or "Jiffy-7" pots and germinate at 75 to 85° F. As soon as the seedlings emerge, reduce the temperature to not less than 60° F., although a minimum of 70° F. is preferred. As soon as the first true leaves have developed, transplant to the beds where they will be grown. Space the plants about 18 in. apart in rows 4 to 5 ft. apart. Use one of the artificial media discussed previously for growing the plants. It is best to grow one of the all-female or "gynoecious" cultivars such as "Rocket" or "Fertila."

Cucumbers should be trellised onto a 6 x 6 in. mesh wire or string netting. This may be vertical if a single row is used, or two rows may be trellised on a "tepee"-type arrangement, with the tops of the trellis being attached to a single supporting framework and the rows about 4 ft. apart. The cucumbers will hang beneath the foliage canopy. For this type of arrangment, it is important that the trellis be 7 to 8 ft. high before joining at the top, to allow room to walk under the canopy for pruning the plants and harvesting the cucumbers.

Pruning and training the vines is important for maximum fruit production. After the plants are transplanted, the main stem should be attached to the supporting trellis. As the plants grow, all lateral branches and flowers are pinched off through the eighth node from the base of the plant. Beginning with the ninth node, all flowers can be left on the main stem and side shoots are allowed to develop but are pinched just beyond the first node on which a flower develops.

There are at least three good reasons for removing side shoots and flowers from the lower 8 nodes of the greenhouse cucumber. One of these is to allow the plant to grow sufficient foliage to support fruit development. The second reason is to have the fruit that are allowed to develop set high enough on the plant so that the fruit does not touch the soil or the artificial medium. Developing fruit should be free of any obstructions, or they are likely to become crooked. A third reason is to prevent too much vegetation, shading, and competition, which would result if all side shoots were left on the plant. As the plants grow, they should be attached to the trellis with plastic clips or twine that is not fastened too tightly around the plant stem.

The hybrid greenhouse cucumber is very prolific when grown under good conditions and may produce 3 or 4 fruit per plant each week during the longer days of late spring and early summer, although as few as 1 or 2 fruit may be expected each week during the short days of midwinter. For the average family, 6 or 8 properly cared for plants should provide plenty of fresh cucumbers for home use.

Fertilizer requirements of greenhouse cucumbers will vary, depending on whether it is a fall crop or a spring crop. As with greenhouse tomatoes, the frequency of fertilizing will usually be closely associated with frequency of watering. As a general rule, the more water a greenhouse crop requires, the greater is the fertilizer requirement. Therefore, as days become longer and warmer, the spring crop would require increasing amounts of fertilizer and water. The opposite is true for the fall crop, since the greatest fertilizer and water requirements would be during late summer and early fall.

Many kinds of fertilizers can be used on greenhouse cucumbers. One of the simplest techniques would be to grow them in one of the peat moss-vermiculite or pine bark-vermiculite combinations discussed in an earlier chapter, and as soon as the first fruit to remain on the plant starts to develop, distribute evenly 6 oz. per plant of Osmocote 14-14-14 on top of the medium. If the 3-month formulation is used, supplemental feeding may be required after the crop has been producing for some time. This may be accomplished by adding 1 oz. of water-soluble 20-20-20 per gal. of water and applying 1 qt. of this solution to each plant at 2- to 3-day intervals for the spring crop and at 7- to 10-day intervals for the fall crop.

If a slow-release fertilizer is not used, it will be necessary to fertilize often. A suggested program to follow for the spring crop is as follows:

Soluble 10-52-17, or similar starter solution, ½ oz. per gal. of water, ½ pt. of solution per plant when transplanted to the bed.

Soluble 20-20-20, 1 oz. per gal. of water, 1 qt. per plant weekly until the first fruits are harvested.

Soluble 20-20-20, 1 oz. per gal. of water, 1 qt. per plant twice weekly for the next 4 weeks.

Soluble 20-20-20, 1 oz. per gal. of water, 1 qt. per plant 3 times each week until harvesting has been completed.

For the fall crop, use 10-52-17 or other high-phosphorus starter fertilizer as for the spring crop at transplanting time. Also, use 20-20-20 at the same dilution and rate of feeding, but not as often as for the spring crop. Twice-weekly feedings might be necessary during the early fruit-production period, but once each week is probably often enough during the short days of midwinter. During periods of prolonged cloudy, dark weather do not use any fertilizer.

The hybrid parthenocarpic cucumber is likely to set more fruit than it can develop, even under ideal growing conditions. Excess fruit will usually turn yellow and drop off while still small. This should be no cause for alarm so long as the color of the leaves and larger fruit is a dark green. However, pale-green fruit and yellowish-green leaves usually indicate a lack of fertilizer, particularly nitrogen. This can be quickly corrected by feeding with water-soluble fertilizer as previously described.

The time interval from flower to harvest of a single fruit may vary from 10 to 20 or more days, depending on growing conditions and the fruit load on the plant. To keep plants productive, all fruit should be harvested as soon as they reach optimal size, usually about 12 to 14 in. long and weighing 12 to 14 oz. When harvesting cucumbers, remove and discard any misshappen fruit or those that have a yellow, shriveled blossom end, in order to promote the growth of the healthy fruit.

If fruit are to be stored for some time before consumption, they should be placed in a plastic bag or wrapped individually in plastic film to prevent dehydration and shriveling. The skin on the parthenocarpic cucumber is very thin and tender, and it is not necessary to peel it. Just wash and slice it into a salad for delicious eating.

Lettuce

Most of the commercially produced lettuce is either the "Boston" or "Butterhead" type or loose-leaf "Grand Rapids." The butterhead or bib type is probably the best for the home greenhouse, since a small space will yield many heads, and a short period of time, 6 to 8 weeks, is all that is required from transplanting until harvest.

Lettuce should be seeded directly into "Jiffy-7" peat pellets, peat pots filled with peat-lite mix, or a seed flat. If seeded in a seed flat, the seedlings should be transplanted to peat pots or other container when they are ½ to ¾ in. high. As soon as the plants are 2 to 3 in. tall they may be transplanted to ground beds. Butterhead or bibb varieties may be spaced 8 x 8 in. and Grand Rapids 12 x 12 in.

One of the best butterhead cultivars is "Butter Crunch," although several other satisfactory bibb varieties are available. For the late-spring or early-summer crop, the more heat-tolerant summer bibb cultivar should be used. Iceberg-type cultivars may be tried, but it is doubtful they would prove superior to the butterhead or Grand Rapids types.

If one of the lightweight soil-less media is used and includes the recommended fertilizer, no additional feeding is usually required for greenhouse lettuce.

Some growers intercrop tomatoes with lettuce. The lettuce is planted around the tomatoes while the tomato plants are small, and, by the time the tomatoes are large enough to shade the lettuce enough to prevent adequate growth, the lettuce is ready to harvest. It is very important to observe the lettuce carefully and remove any lower leaves that become infected with gray mold (botrytis).

Greenhouse lettuce is a high-quality food but must be harvested at the proper stage to prevent quality deterioration. Some experi-

Bottom heat is essential for the rooting of many types of cuttings and the germination of many seeds. The soil-warming cables are buried in sand and the seeds or cuttings grown in either pots or soil above the sand. The temperature is thermostatically controlled. *Courtesy of Humex.*

ence is necessary to determine when to harvest, but with the butterhead varieties, do not wait too long. Begin harvesting as soon as the center "semi-head" is 3 in. or so in diameter. Late-spring and early-summer crops are likely to develop seedstalks, called "bolting." As soon as stem elongation begins, quality deteriorates rapidly. Start harvesting before this begins.

Root crops

Carrots, beets, and radishes may also be grown in the greenhouse. These should be sown in rows 4 to 6 in. apart and the seed covered ¼ to ½ in. deep. After emergence, the seedlings should be thinned to 10 or 12 per ft. of row, and, upon reaching

Tomatoes are one of the most rewarding greenhouse food crops. Although not difficult to grow, they need quite a lot of attention throughout the growing season.

edible size, they may be pulled and used as needed. Actually, radishes may be left 15 to 20 per ft. of row, and, as the larger ones are removed, smaller ones will continue to grow. Most of the cultivars suitable for outdoor use should be suitable in the greenhouse. Three or 4 of row of radishes and 8 to 10 ft. of row of carrots or beets at each planting should provide an adequate supply for the average family. A new planting of radishes should be made when the first harvest is made from the latest planting.

Green onions may be easily grown in the greenhouse from seed or sets. Two or 3 plantings will usually provide a continuous supply of green onions throughout the fall, winter, and spring months. Much less time is required to grow green onions if they are grown from sets. However, a combination of seed and sets may be the most practical, with seed being planted during late summer for the fall and winter crops and sets being planted during the winter for spring use.

Cultivars suitable for use include sweet ''Spanish,'' ''Ebenezer,'' and ''Beltsville bunching.'' Plant seed ¼ in. deep in rows 6 in. apart. Thin seedlings to ½ in. apart. Further thinning may be done as the onions become large enough for consumption. Sets should be planted 1½ in. deep, 1 in. apart, and in rows 6 in. apart.

Snap beans

In a lean-to greenhouse, snap beans are a good crop to grow against the back wall, if the pole-types are used. The pole beans are suggested because they take advantage of the vertical space in a greenhouse, whereas the bush types hug the ground and do not give as much yield per square foot of space used. Sow the seed in peat pots in February or March and plant them into the bed when they are 4 to 6 in. tall. Allow about 18 in. between plants. Two good, old-time favorite cultivars are ''Blue Lake'' and ''Kentucky Wonder.'' Grow them on stakes or on twine. Fertilize as for cucumbers. Keep the leafhoppers and red spider mites under control. On very warm days after the plants begin to bloom, an occasional light misting will improve the pod set.

Sweet peas grow well in the greenhouse and provide almost continuous bloom. A wide range of cultivars are available.

If you prefer the bush types, they can be grown as well, but they should be placed to get adequate light. Sow the seed directly into the bed, 2 to 3 in. apart in rows 12 in. apart. Any cultivar you prefer may be grown.

Keep the temperature above 60° F. and ventilate during the day if the temperature exeeds 85° F.

Lima beans are sometimes grown in the greenhouse but are not recommended for the amateur, since this plant is very difficult to get to set pods well under poor light conditions.

Other forcing crops

Asparagus. Lift well-developed plants into a 60° F. greenhouse and pack them together under a 3-in. layer of damp peat moss under a greenhouse bench. With plenty of moisture, the spears will quickly appear. Spears may be harvested for up to 8 weeks, and then the plants should be moved outside to store up food materials for next year's crop. In general practice, however, the spears are usually harvested for as long as they are producing well, and then the crowns are discarded. Asparagus crowns should not be brought into the greenhouse before early February.

Rhubarb. This is perhaps the easiest of all vegetables to force. In November or December, lift well-developed crowns. Let them become thoroughly frosted; trim the root ball; then move them into a 45 or 50° F. greenhouse. Place them close together in peat under a bench where they will be in as complete darkness as possible. Water heavily. It is the leaf petiole that is eaten, and the cooler the temperature, the redder will be the petioles. *The leaf blade is extremely poisonous and should never be eaten.*

Endive, parsley, chinese cabbage and **turnip greens.** These crops are sometimes grown in the greenhouse to satisfy some special desire, and they do well at night temperatures of 55° F. Grow directly in the beds or in large pots.

With a little experience, you will find you can grow most any vegetable crop in the greenhouse, although it is impractical to produce any kind that can be grown outside and stored, or to try to grow those that require a great deal of space.

9 Propagation

Sowing seeds — Vegetative propagation — Pricking off and potting

Despite its technical sound, the word propagation simply means regenerating new plants by planting seeds, taking cuttings, dividing up old plants, or other methods. A greenhouse is far from essential to the propagation process, but, because its environment is protected and controlled, it will not only speed up the process but will give you greater success and widen the range of plants that you can multiply to include a whole galaxy of tender and half-hardy species that need the warmth your greenhouse can offer.

Whatever the kind of propagation you have in mind, you must be able to give newly developing plants air, moisture, and the right temperature. There is no infallible method that will bring success. Often trial and error is the quickest way of progress, but there are some general rules which you should stick to.

Sowing seeds

Growing plants from seed is cheap and gives good results, but do resist the temptation to collect your own seeds from plants you have grown in the greenhouse. Rather, buy from a reputable dealer. The reason for this is that flowers that are fertilized with pollen from another plant may not breed true.

While some seeds, like those of the cucumber, germinate very quickly and easily, others, like primula seeds, are very difficult to germinate. One reason for this is a very hard seed coat, which acts as a barrier and prevents water from reaching the embryo within; another reason is that the seed may naturally have a long resting or dormancy period. For hard-coated seeds, the best treatment is to dip them into hot water before you plant them, as this will soften them and allow water in. To break the dormancy, put the seeds into a refrigerator for a few weeks before taking them into a warm greenhouse.

The best substance to grow seeds in, whatever their size or shape, is any medium that retains water and is well aerated. Mixtures of peat with sand, perlite, or vermiculite are good. The container you choose will depend on how many seeds you plan to plant. For small batches use clay or plastic seed "pans" or bowls, for large ones seed flats are best. Plastic seed trays are probably the best choice, as they are so simple to clean and do not rot, and these are sometimes attached to plastic covers to make small propagating units.

If you are using a box for planting, fill the bottom with some roughage like rough peat before you add the medium. Clay pots will need some pieces of crock put over the drainage hole. Other containers can be filled directly with the medium. Add it up to the rim, make sure it is damp, and press it down with a piece of wood so that the surface is even. Water well and allow it to drain, or stand the container is a shallow tray containing an inch or so of water for a few minutes.

The best way to sow fine seed is to scatter it thinly on the surface, then press it in lightly. Hold the container at eye level to make sure of even sowing. Larger seeds can be scattered over the surface, then covered with some more medium rubbed through a fine screen. A method that has been tried and tested by gardeners for years is to put the seeds into a piece of cardboard folded down the middle. If you prefer to plant with "finger and thumb," remember that fine seeds will stick to your fingers. Large seeds can merely be pressed into the medium.

Try to sow as thinly as you can, and, after sowing, *always* give seeds a very light watering with a very fine spray. Then cover them with a sheet of glass with paper on top. This keeps the humidity high and traps moisture. Light is unnecessary and often undesirable for germination.

The ideal temperature for germination varies from species to species, but 55 to 60° F. will suit the majority, although begonias need about 10° more than this. Look at the seed containers often to make sure they are not dry, and turn the glass over every day so that drops of water do not soak the compost. As soon as you see signs of germination, remove the paper and lift the glass a little to ventilate. For the next few days keep the seedlings out of bright sunlight, even if you have to protect them with a sheet of paper. Finally, if you have the facilities, you might like to imitate the commercial growers and keep the greenhouse at high humidity and a temperature of 75° F. for a few days, in which time many seeds will germinate.

Vegetative propagation

As its name suggests, vegetative propagation involves taking some part of the plant and inducing it to make roots. These cuttings may be from the stem, leaves, or the roots themselves, or may be in the form of a bulb, a runner, or a tuber. In general, the plants whose roots grow closest to the surface of the ground are easiest to propagate: the chrysanthemum is a good example.

The most favorable time for taking cuttings is the season when the plant is growing most rapidly. For Plants with soft wood, such as dahlias and chrysanthemums, this will be early in the year when the new season's growth has begun. The cuttings do, however, need high temperatures — between 60 and 65° F. — to form roots.

Pelargoniums, hydrangeas, and many other shrubs with moderate amounts of wood are best propagated later in the year. They can be rooted at lower temperatures; that is, from 50 to 55° F. Woody plants, such as roses, give the best cuttings in fall and will form roots at low temperatures, but the vital rooting process will be speeded up considerably in the warmth of the greenhouse.

Usually, the tips of the side shoots, or sometimes the end of the main growing shoot, make the best cuttings, but reject any plants that show signs of disease. Be certain your cuttings are as healthy as possible. Snapping the cutting off cleanly by hand will cut down the risk of spreading fungi or viruses, but, if you prefer to use a knife, choose one with a sharp, narrow blade or employ a fairly new razor blade.

The best length for a cutting is 2 or 3 in., although many plants can be propagated from long cuttings bearing three or four buds. Put the cuttings in boxes, seed pans, or open beds that you have filled with a rooting medium. This can be sand, peat, a mixture of the two, or one of peat and vermiculite. Or you can use the new compressed-peat pellets, which do away with the need for transplanting later on. Make holes with a pencil, and put the cuttings in 1 to 3 in. apart, having dusted them, with hormone rooting powder according to the maker's directions.

Two common greenhouse plants, the rex begonias and saintpaulia, are often propagated by taking leaf cuttings. For the begonias, take off a large leaf and make some cuts across the leaf veins, then place it on some rooting medium. Some gardeners put small stones over the cuts, but this is not essential. Take saintpaulia leaves with the stem attached and simply stand them in the rooting medium. Both these sorts of leaf cuttings thrive in high humidity.

All cuttings will make roots more quickly if you can set up some sort of humid, enclosed atmosphere. This may merely be a plastic bag attached to a stick covering the pot, or it may be a mist propagating unit that carefully controls heat and moisture. Plastic propagating cases, consisting of a tray and a transparent cover, are very effective. Maintain the temperature of the greenhouse at a level that can be kept similar to that of the rooting medium. A temperature between 55 and 60° F. is acceptable for most plants.

Kalanchoe blossfeldiana. An attractive, long-lasting flowering plant for home deco-
ration. Seed germinates in 7 to 10 days at 65° F. Seed sown in May produces
flowering plants from January to spring. For Christmas flowering, give short-day
treatment, beginning September 20 to 25 for 4 weeks.

Pricking off and potting

Once seedlings are well grown and cuttings are obviously rooting and established in the growing medium, both can be transferred or pricked off to boxes or pots of the right size. Do not use pots that are too large as they take up too much greenhouse space. Remember that plants in clay or plastic pots will need repotting, while those in peat or bituminized paper pots can be transplanted in their entirety.

To avoid damaging the leaves or roots, gently tease seedlings out of their germination trays with a dibble. Look at the roots to make sure they are not diseased — they should be white, not brown — then make a hole in the new medium with your dibble, and plant the seedling. Then firm it in. If you are pricking off into standard boxes, put 8 seedlings per row in 6 rows, and try to have some sort of grading system according to size. If you are using soil blocks, you will have to add extra compost to fill up the voids between them. Once they have been planted and firmed in, give them a good watering.

Cuttings can be handled very much like seedlings, and both must be kept at a favorable temperature of around 60° F. Many gardeners think that in winter open benches give the plants a better start, but a closed-in situation will be better in summer, as the plants will then need less watering.

The time for the next repotting or for planting out will depend on how quickly the new plants grow and how many roots they make. Moving a plant into a larger pot is quite simple. Choose a pot 2 in. larger in diameter. Put a little roughage in the bottom and partly fill it with soil. Take the small pot containing the plant, turn it upside down, and tap the base lightly. Cup the ball of the roots in your hand as the plants comes out, so that is does not disintegrate, then put in the soil layer in the new pot. Fill the pot to within ½ in. of the rim, and press in firmly if the plant is shrubby or woody, less firmly if it is soft and succulent. At every stage take the trouble to label the plants clearly and carefully.

All plants that will eventually flower or fruit outdoors must be gradually accustomed to temperatures outside the greenhouse. This hardening-off process is ideally accomplished in a cold frame, but a sunny, sheltered spot will do. In a frame, give more and more air each day until April or May when there is no chance of a late frost.

10 Diseases, Insects and Other Problems

In the congenial atmosphere of the greenhouse, plants grow quickly, but so do all kinds of insects and diseases, and the less the greenhouse environment is controlled, the more rampant these pests will be. Control of the greenhouse environment, however, is not the whole answer, and while modern chemical controls can be most effective, many organisms have built up a resistance to these compounds.

Just as the human body is made more vulnerable by the extremes of cold and heat, so greenhouse plants will be attacked more easily if you give them too much or too little food, excess or lack of water, if you overheat the greenhouse or forget to turn on the heat. Hygiene is important, too. Many pests and diseases are so small that they are invisible to the naked eye, but regularly disinfecting your equipment with detergent will control them.

Warning

If you use chemical pesticides and insecticides, *always* follow the manufacturer's instructions to the letter. Fumigants need particularly careful handling. *Lock all these substances away* out of the reach of children. The chemical DDT is often referred to in gardening books but is no longer available, as it has been judged injurious to man and animals. New chemicals for controlling insects and diseases are constantly coming on the market. Follow the recommendations of the County Extension Agent on the pesticides to use in the garden.

TEMPERATURE CONVERSION TABLES

°F	°C	°F	°C
86	30.0	65	18.3
85	29.4	64	17.8
84	28.9	63	17.2
83	28.3	62	16.7
82	27.8	61	16.1
81	27.2	60	15.6
80	26.7	59	15.0
79	26.1	58	14.4
78	25.6	57	13.9
77	25.0	56	13.3
76	24.4	55	12.8
75	23.9	54	12.2
74	23.3	53	11.7
73	22.8	52	11.1
72	22.2	51	10.6
71	21.7	50	10.0
70	21.1	49	9.4
69	20.6	48	8.9
68	20.0	47	8.3
67	19.4	46	7.8
66	18.9	45	7.2

SOME FACTS AND FIGURES

8,000 seeds are contained in 1 oz. of tomato seed
1 ton of soil mix contains approximately 36 bushels
A bushel measures 22 x 10 x 10 in.
1 bushel of soil = 1¼ cubic feet
16 fl. oz. = 1 pint
1 tablespoon = ½ fl. oz.
3 teaspoons = 1 tablespoon

Formula for conversion:

Centigrade to Fahrenheit = $(°C \times \frac{9}{5}) + 32$

Fahrenheit to Centigrade = $(°F - 32) \times \frac{5}{9}$

Diseases, Insects, and Problems

CROP, PLANT OR GREENHOUSE	DISORDERS	SYMPTOMS	PREVENTION AND CONTROL
General propagation, seed sowing, rooting cuttings, culture of young plants, bedding plants, etc.	Damping off; Pythium Spp; Rhizocotonia Spp., Phytophthora Spp. of cut part or at compost level.	Base of seedlings and young plants turns light brown and stem constricts. Plant eventually collapses. Cuttings attacked in area of cut part or at compost level.	Cheshunt compound can be used before sowing and also for newly germinated seedlings. Zineb or PCNB can also be used, as instructed on product, as can captan dust or spray
General propagation, seed sowing, rooting cuttings, culture of young plants, bedding plants, etc.	Gray mold	Attacks cuttings or young plants. Starts as light-brown lesion, eventually becoming covered with gray, dust-like spores	Encouraged by high humidity. Especially troublesome in a greenhouse that is allowed to chill overnight. Use Thiram dust as directed or use Captan
Bulbs and corms; carnations, chrysanthemums, cucumbers, pot plants tomatoes, lettuce, and crops in general	Aphids of various species. Small flies can be seen on leaves, usually in clusters	Attack leaves, feeding on plant sap, causing distortion and loss of vigor. Virus disease can also be transmitted by various species	Use insecticidal spray, atomizing fluid, smoke at first sign of attack, changing the nature of the chemical frequently, if possible, to avoid build-up of resistance
Bulbs and corms; chrysanthemums, tomatoes, and several other crops	Caterpillars; Angle shade moth; Tomato moth	Caterpillars feeding on leaves and flowers, often at night	Use pesticides recommended by the County Extension Agent.
Bulbs and corms; chrysanthemums	Stem eelworm (Ditylenchus dipsaci) attacks bulbs and other plants. Chrysanthemums attacked by specific eelworm (Apelenchoides ritzems-bosi)	Attack leaves and flowers, causing distortion. In chrysanthemums brown blotches are formed on leaves, changing from yellow to bronze and purple	Destroy stock of bulbs and use only fresh soil in future. Chrysanthemums' stools can be hot-water treated — 115° F. for 5 min.
Narcissus (daffodils)	Narcissus flies	Eggs laid in or near bulbs in spring. Produce larvae that tunnel into bulbs, resulting in failure after planting	Bulb suppliers generally ensure that all bulbs are free from infestation by hot-water treatment or chemical dipping.

CROP, PLANT OR GREENHOUSE	DISORDERS	SYMPTOMS	PREVENTION AND CONTROL
Narcissus (daffodils)	Leaf scorch (Stagonospora curtisii)	Leaf tip turns reddish brown, followed by death	Spray with Zineb at first sign of attack and repeat several times.
Bulbs and corms; carnations, chrysanthemums, cucumbers, pot plants generally, tomatoes, inside shrubs	Thrips of various species, small brown or yellowish insects	Attack plants in various ways —sucking sap from leaves or flowers, causing acute distortion of growth. Silvery spots often show, especially on carnations. Breeding is more or less continuous	Malathion and Nicotine, applied repeatedly until control is gained
Carnations, chrysanthemums, lettuce, tomatoes	Wireworms (small ½-¾ in. yellow-bodied insects)	Eggs laid in May/July. Larvae hatch in a few weeks and eat roots of plants. Persist for 4-5 years	Apply insecticide
Tomatoes, carnations	Fusarium wilt (Fusarium oxysporum and F. dianthi and other species).	Carnations and tomatoes are affected in warm areas. Plants wilt and die	Use resistant cultivars and sterilized soil.
All crops	Grey mold (Botrytis cinerea)	Attacks a wide range of plants, causing discoloration of leaves, followed by gray dust-like mold. Spreads extremely rapidly. Tomatoes badly attacked on stems, leaves or fruit. Ghost spot on fruit is caused by partial development of botrytis. Lettuce can also be badly attacked.	Keep atmosphere dry by ventilation and application of heat. Avoid severe night temperature drops. Use fungicide

Carnations	Carnation fly	Eggs laid on upper surface of leaves, resulting in larvae that moves into the stem	Use insecticide
Tulips	"Fire" (Botrytis tulipae)	Deformed shoots, followed by gray spots that eventually run together, resulting in reddish discoloration of leaves	Zineb, Thiram, or PCNB sprays or dust used at first sign of attack and persisted with
Many crops and plants	Earwigs	Bite holes in flowers and stems during night, causing acute distortion and malformation	Trap with inverted pots
Many crops and plants	Red spider mite (Tetranychus urticae and T. cinnebarinus)	Nymphs and adults suck sap from leaves, causing yellowing and eventual destruction of leaves. Webs develop on underside of leaves, hindering control	Extremely persistent pests, overwintering in cracks in greenhouse. A variety of materials should be used as smokes or sprays to avoid building up resistance
Carnations, chrysanthemums, pot plants, and shrubs	Powdery mildew (Oidium sp.)	Dirty white powder on leaves, stems, and flowers	
Carnations, chrysanthemums, and other plants	Rust (Uromyces dianthi)	Small blotches on leaves, later releasing reddish-brown spores	Thiram, Zineb sprays or dusts, at first sign of disease. Overwinters in stools of chrysanthemums.
Carnations	Stem rot (Fusarium culmorum), Verticillium wilt (Verticillium cinerescens)	Soil-borne disease enters roots and spreads up plant, affecting moisture-conducting tissue. Wilt follows, sometimes only on one side of plant on carnations	Adequate soil sterilization by heat or effective chemicals. Raising greenhouse temperature to 75° F. for a week, combined with surface mulching, can offset trouble

Plant(s)	Pest/Disease	Description	Control
Tomatoes	Verticillium wilt (Verticillium alboatrum)		
Chrysanthemums	Gall midge (Diarthronomyia chrysanthemi)	Cone-shaped galls form on leaves and stems	Use insecticides
Chrysanthemums, pot plants, tomatoes	Leaf miner (Phytomyza and Liriomyza solani)	Eggs laid on leaves produce larvae that tunnel into leaves	Use insecticides
Chrysanthemums	Tarnished plant bug or capsid (Lygus rugulipennis)	Bugs suck sap, exuding toxin that twists and distorts. A wide range of plants are attacked outdoors	Use insecticides
Chrysanthemums, cucumbers, melons, pot plants, tomatoes	White Fly (Trialeurodes vaporariorum)	Eggs laid on leaves, hatching into nymphs that suck sap and exude honeydew on which molds develop. Growth is distorted. In pelargoniums leaf spot may be spread by this pest	A variety of sprays, dusts, aerosols, or smokes can be used. Thorough cleaning or fumigating of greenhouse in winter when empty is essential

118

CROP, PLANT OR GREENHOUSE	DISORDERS	SYMPTOMS	PREVENTION AND CONTROL
Chrysanthemums	Blotch or leaf spot (Spetoria chrysanthemella)	Gray or black blotches on leaves, often confused with eelworm	Spray with Zineb
Chrysanthemums	Petal damping, botrytis, gray mold	"Pin-pointing" of flower, followed by complete flower rot	Improve environment by application of heat, especially at night
Chrysanthemums	Petal blight (Itersonilia spp.)	Affects outside petals as water spots and spreads into flower center	Zineb spray or dust before bud bursting
Chrysanthemums	Ray blight (Mycosphaerella ligulicola)	Mainly attacks inside when growing chrysanthemums on year-round culture	Obtain clean stock. Spray with Zineb. Difficult to control once in existence
Cucumbers, melons tomatoes	Leafhoppers (Erythroneura pallidifrons)	Lively insects feeding on leaves cause distortion and restrict growth	Use insecticides
Cucumber	Fungus gnats of various species	Develop initially on decaying fungi or straw bales. Attack roots of plants, causing wilting or death	Use insecticides
Cucumbers, melons and other soft plants	Springtails of various species	White, six-legged soil pests feeding on soft stems; roots, and root hairs in clusters. Some actively jump by means of tails	Use insecticides
Cucumbers, melons, lettuce, tomatoes, and practically all other plants	Symphylid (Scutigerella immaculata)	Very active ¼ in. long insects feeding on roots, causing hard or deformed growth. They move down to lower depths of soil in winter or when soil is wet. Worst in highly organic soil	Thoroughly sterilize soild by heat or effective chemicals. Use insecticides
Cucumbers	Black rot (Mycosphaerella citrullina)	Dieback of laterals at main stem. Identified by small black spots	Zineb spray, coupled with sterilization of boxes, etc., to avoid spread of infection

Cucumbers	Gummosis (Cladosporium cucumerinum)	Silver spots on fruit, which turn gummy, followed by velvety growth of green fungus	Use fungicide
Cucumbers	Powdery mildew	White felt over leaves	Use fungicide
Lettuce	Millipedes, various species	Many-legged 1 in. long creatures attacking roots and stems	Normally feed on organic matter. Adequate soil sterilization
Lettuce, pot plants	Downy mildew	Yellow areas on upper surface of leaves with gray fungus on correspondingly lower areas	Use fungicide
Pot plants, peaches, nectarines, vines	Mealybug (Pseudococcus spp.)	Little bugs covered with waxy secretion cluster on plants and cause distortion or loss of vigor, followed by leaf loss	Use insecticide
Primulas, auriculas, lettuce	Root aphis (Pemphigus auriculae and other sp.)	Clusters of waxy-like insects present on the roots	Use insecticide
Vines, cyclamens, and other plants	Vine weevil (Otiorrhynchus sulcatus)	Eggs laid in soil hatch in 2-3 weeks and white grubs feed on roots, causing wilting	Use insecticide
Cyclamen	Root and corm rots (Cylindrocarpon radicola and Thielviopsis basicoli)	Soil-borne disease that attacks and rots corms and roots	Use sterilized compost. Zineb drench is also effective
Tomatoes	Potato root eelworm (Heterodera rostochiensis)	Resting cysts start early in season, releasing minute larvae that attack root systems, causing browning of lower leaves and wilting of plant. Their activities allow entry of root rots and other diseases	Very difficult to gain complete control in tomato borders. Alternative methods of cultivation allowing isolation from borders, using sterilized media, are advisable in bad cases

CROP, PLANT OR GREENHOUSE	DISORDERS	SYMPTOMS	PREVENTION AND CONTROL
Tomatoes	Root-knot eelworm (Meloidogyne spp.)	Roots attacked, resulting in a deformed and galled appearance. Will rest in soil for 2 years in absence of host plants	Sterilize the soil
Tomatoes	Buckeye rot	Soil-borne spores splash onto fruit, causing disfiguring dark-brown rings	Take great care when watering, avoid splashing. Adequate ventilation will also help. Spray with fungicide at first sign of attack
Tomatoes	Leaf mold (Cladosporium fulvum)	Starts as yellow spots on upper surface, with corresponding gray-brown mold patches on lower surfaces. Appearance of disease coincides with periods of still muggy weather when humidity is high. Once established, it can spread rapidly and affect flowers as well as leaves. Has an overall yield-reducing effect	Certain districts are notorious for this disease, especially those where humidity is high. It is always advisable to grow resistant varieties in bad areas When nonresistant varieties are grown, spray with fungicide. Good ventilation night and day, coupled with adequate air movement by means of fans or use of heaters, will do much to offset the trouble
Tomatoes	Potato blight (Phytophthora infestans)	More common in the south where tomatoes are grown outdoors. Brown sunken areas appear on fruit	The same control measures as described for leaf mold should be practiced
Tomatoes	Root and foot rot (Phytophthora spp.; Pythium spp., Rhizoctonia solani)	Fungi enter through roots or base of stem, especially when plants are subjected to growing checks or soils are unusually wet or previously badly contaminated	Soil sterilization for the future is essential. Fungicide can be used at 3-4 week intervals. Avoid checks to growth (especially planting in cold soil)
Tomatoes	Sclerotinia disease (Sclerotinia sclerotiorum)	Only Base of stems attacked. A white mold develops, followed by black resting bodies. Plants wilt and die	Special attention should be paid to sterilization for the future

PHYSIOLOGICAL DISORDERS

TOMATOES

Blossom end rot	End of fruit develops a black zone	Caused by inadequate or irregular watering, too high a salt content, or not enough limestone in soil
Cracking or splitting of fruit	Fruit cracks or splits	Due to widely varying environmental conditions and may largely be influenced by type of weather. Sometimes due to boron deficiency
Dry set and blossom drop	Flowers fall off or fruit fails to set	Due to irregular growing conditions, especially temperatures below 65° F. and above 80° F., also perhaps to virus infection
Blotchy ripening	Irregular ripening of fruit	Caused by day temperatures being too high and by irregular feeding. Give regular liquid feeds and keep potash level high. Do not overwater

POT PLANTS

Overwatering	Yellow and wilting of lower leaves	Always ensure that plants are not overwatered by constant supervision. Sometimes low night temperature has the same effect
Overfeeding over-fertilizing	Scorched appearance of foliage and leaf tips	Apply less fertilizer or in more diluted form

MANY PLANTS

Gross, lanky length	Lack of light	Make sure that plants obtain maximum light, especially in winter, bearing in mind their likes and dislikes in this direction

121